Mindfulness for the Family

A PARENT-CHILD WORKBOOK
FOR GREATER AWARENESS AND
STRONGER RELATIONSHIPS

Kathirasan K and Sunita Rai

Marshall Cavendish Editions

For our parents, who guided and supported us.

For our siblings, who have made our lives colourful and bright.

For all parents, teachers, fosterers, caregivers and guardians of young minds.

And for parents-to-be.

Contents

CHAPTER 1

Introduction

On a Sunday evening we were out for a stroll in a beautiful park right in the centre of Singapore. There is a small river that runs through this park. It attracts migratory birds, water lizards, otters, turtles and many kinds of fish, including the occasional African Sharptooth walking catfish. Different migratory birds visit this river over the year, and we believe they travelled thousands of miles to get here.

The river has a total of three large bridges, as well as two stepping stones that allow people to cross the river where the water depth is usually low. As we were heading towards one of those stepping stones, we noticed two families with children actively engaged in the knee-deep river. We were curious and decided to pay attention to what they were doing.

The parents in one family were teaching the kids how to fish with handheld nets. The kids were very excited trying to catch the tiny fish which usually linger at the edge of the river. The other family was doing something else. The parents in this family were teaching the kids to feed the fish in the river. They were feeding pieces of bread and watching the shoal of tilapias having a feast on them.

This incident immediately brought a very interesting insight to our minds: the idea of consumption and contribution. We saw life as an interplay of consumption and contribution, but sometimes one can dominate our lives more than the other.

Our love for our children and our family members are also subject to this interplay of two energies. As families, we tend to spend a lot of energy and time in consuming but seldom do we think about contributing as a family. We might do it individually but perhaps not collectively as a family.

At times we may think about contribution, especially when it comes to taking care of ourselves or the people we love. But what we are talking about here in terms of contribution is the way that we can bring value to ourselves and our family, to others in our community and the world as well.

The incident at the park created the desire in us to see if we can inspire family cultures that balance these two energies. Being mindfulness practitioners and teachers, this incident prompted us to look at family life from a mindfulness perspective.

The second reason was another incident that similarly helped us shape our thoughts in this book. We have spent many years teaching in various tertiary institutions. I (Kathir) was teaching a class where budding teenagers were learning professional skills to become successful in their lives.

In one of the classes I enquired into their well-being. Immediately, many of the students shared that they were leading miserable lives. Being the curious person I am, I wanted to find out the reason. The teenagers shared that their parents did not love them and all that they were interested in was their grades.

This came as a surprise to me because these teenagers were living in a first-world country, with close to luxurious lives, and yet were feeling that they were not good enough. Their purpose and meaning were quite different from what their parents wanted them to be.

While education is very important, it is not the only thing that defines a person's value. These teenagers were clearly very unhappy that they were being measured by or valued for their grades.

I (Sunita) had a similar experience while teaching my group of 18–19-year-old teenagers on the subject on human relationships. I have been teaching in tertiary institutions for over ten years and whenever my students and I discuss the topic of family communication and attachment, a consistent pattern of comments emerges.

What were their comments? 'My parents never listen.' 'My mother only wants me to score well.' 'My parents are always comparing me with others.' 'My father only cares about me being the top student.' 'Communication is one-way in our family: parents to me. They don't listen.' And the list goes on.

You can see from here that many youths feel that they are judged by their academic achievements and that they are not listened to. It is the same even with the younger children I've worked with. Children and teenagers feel disconnected from the expectations of their parents. I remember one of the boys in a children's shelter that I was working in commenting that the staff always greeted him with the same question, 'What is your homework for today?', instead of asking him about his day or health.

These incidents reveal something significant about our priorities and what is meaningful to us. When we do not know what is meaningful and important to us – what makes our lives worth living – then we may end up being motivated by values that are not intrinsic to us. These could be values that we have imposed on ourselves through the eyes of others.

For example, having the desire to live in a mansion at some point in our life could be due to a friend who lived in a mansion and seemed happier than us. It is common and not necessarily unhealthy to ascribe value to things through the lenses of others but only if the values are shared. And we as adults unconsciously pass these values and behaviours to the people we live with, especially children.

One of my clients shared during a psychotherapy session that he was 'only' earning S$400,000 a year. According to statistics, the average income of Singaporeans is $3,940 a month, which works out to be about $47,280 a year. At $400,000, he was probably among the top 2–3% of earners in Singapore.

So I inquired deeper into his relationship with money and the value he placed on money. He proceeded to tell me about his father's expectations of him from a young age. In many of my psychotherapy cases, it always boils down to the values and morals that people pick up in their early years. This is another reason why mindfulness is important to families.

What we want is for children to learn to find values from within themselves and not let it be something that is created as a result of another's values. These intrinsic values will guide their lives and help them clarify what is meaningful and purposeful for them.

Our Families

The two of us (Kathir and Sunita) had very similar childhoods. We lived with our respective siblings, often with little privacy. There were times when money was a challenge. Our parents (Sunita) and grandparents (Kathir) had come from India to Singapore to find means of living comfortably. While they were landowners back in India, in Singapore they had to work as employees in harsh conditions.

My (Kathir) maternal grandfather's plan was to earn as much money in Singapore so that he could grow his assets in India. However, his fate turned out quite differently. He got married to my grandmother here and started a family. He had eleven children, and that rendered his dream impossible. What he earned was only sufficient for his family. But after all his children got married and started their own families, he returned to India, where he spent has final years.

My father worked in the British Royal Navy base in Singapore all his life. My mother was primarily a homemaker who sometimes took a part-time job to make ends meet. They had two children, my elder sister and me. I had a happy childhood even though we lived a frugal life in a two-bedroom government apartment.

My childhood was spent in neighbourhood schools, playing soccer with my schoolmates and listening to lots of music because my father was a music fan as well as a musician. We lived a comfortable life until my father passed away due to a road accident when I was 13. That left my family in grief for many years and caused a rift to grow between us. We seldom spoke, and my sister and I would have frequent squabbles. But all this changed when my sister got married and our family life became positive again.

Personally, it was mindfulness that lifted me out of the effects of this period in my early adult life. I wish we as a family had learned these practices earlier on so that we could have coped with the grief and unhappiness.

My (Sunita) father left India for similar reasons as Kathir's grandfather. He was the youngest of five children and came to Singapore when he was about 14 years old. His parents had passed away when he was very young and he had been brought up by his siblings, so he naturally felt indebted to them and wanted to earn money to send back to India.

He did very well in that regard, in my opinion. He was able to help his relatives when in need, restore dilapidated schools and even finance the restoration of small temples in his hometown. His plan was to eventually return to India after making enough money and settling his children in Singapore.

But that did not happen because he was a victim of an accident which affected his brain and eventually brought on a stroke. He only returned to India once after his stroke to finish completing a temple, which he had vowed to do, and my mother assisted him in his journey and completing his vows. He passed away in Singapore in 2016 without fulfilling his dream of returning to his hometown.

Our stories are classic in the sense that what our parents or grandparents planned was quite different from what happened in reality. After I (Kathir) lost my father, I was brought up by my mother singlehandedly, along with my sister, who was older than me by 5 years. She struggled for many years to help us feel like a complete family and put us through our education. While she shared her grief at losing her husband, she never once complained about struggling for us.

I (Sunita) grew up with four siblings, who were all older than me. Money was always tight for us. My father was the sole breadwinner and he worked two jobs and was away 24/7. Both my parents were illiterate but wanted all their children to have an education, as they felt that education was the only way out of poverty as well as a way of influencing others. My father provided for us financially as much as he could but I barely knew him as a person because he was seldom at home. My mother was usually so busy caring for all of us that she hardly cared for herself.

Our lives were basically comfortable but in a very different way from the comfort that we are experiencing today. 'Comfort' can range from a simple life where basic needs are met, to a life of luxury.

For both of us, childhood was filled with playing games with siblings, neighbours and friends at school. Family time was spent watching movies and documentaries together. The value of being in a family was implicitly seen as being supportive of each other, valuing each other's presence and being happy.

Occasionally we would have guests visit our homes without notice, which is an uncommon practice these days. Our parents never complained about unexpected guests. There is a famous dictum in the Indian tradition where guests are to be treated like gods. We have seen our mothers finding time in between preparing meals to entertain the guests. They ensured that guests had the best possible experience in our homes.

Although we had very little, we learned to live happily with what we had. My (Sunita) siblings would pass down clothes, toys and books so that my parents did not have to buy new things for each child. And we shared what we had.

But there were also times when we found ourselves unhappy or confused or angry. Looking back, if we had known about mindfulness practices then, we would have been much better at dealing with some of these unhealthy emotions.

For example, as children, we had to live by our parents' values. These were non-negotiable, and rarely explained to us. We had to follow them even if we didn't necessarily understand the rationale for them. Such values would have included respecting our elders, speaking the truth, not hurting others, helping those in need, and sharing what we had.

I (Sunita) remember when I was very young, being angry with my father once for agreeing to help someone financially when we did not have enough for ourselves. I did not understand his values then. Now I understand, but perhaps it would have been more impactful if we had been told the value and reasons behind his actions.

Not adhering to our parents' expectations resulted in punishments, which were corporal at times. The occasional mindfulness activities that I (Sunita) experienced revolved around spiritual activities that we were not able to comprehend. We also wrongly assumed that mindfulness could only be learned from a religious practice. With the dawn of secular mindfulness, every family and every individual can benefit from these practices.

Our childhoods taught us the importance of lived wisdom, or wisdom in action. Often, we may think that wisdom is contained in books or that it belongs to philosophers. But wisdom is way more powerful when it takes place dynamically in our lives. For example, talking about the value of speaking the truth when a child has uttered a lie is not as important as living the value by speaking the truth at all times. Lived wisdom is perhaps the most powerful attribute in mindful families.

I (Kathir) have been interested in mindfulness philosophies and insights for more than 25 years. In 1999, I met my mindfulness teacher for the first time. I spent 6 years with him studying and learning the practices of mindfulness philosophy and practices through the source texts in Sanskrit. Since then, mindfulness has been my anchor and compass, keeping me grounded and guiding me through life.

Having been trained in both spiritual and secular evidence-based mindfulness, I am able to present both forms with strict distinction, based on the audience and their needs. Each has its place and goals. When teaching secular mindfulness, one should be clear that one does not bring spiritual ideas into it – that is my belief.

I (Sunita) was first exposed to mindfulness in 2005 during my undergraduate studies in psychology, but it was only in 2007 that I delved deeper into its ideas and practices. My training in spiritual meditation, secular evidence-based mindfulness, psychology and counselling have provided me with a strong theoretical and experiential foundation.

This grounding, together with my years of experience in the field of psychotherapy, is one of the reasons why I always say that mindfulness, while it has many benefits, is not a magic pill. Medication, psychotherapy, counselling, coaching and mindfulness amongst others have their own place and purpose. I use many of the mindfulness practices in my work as a consultant, psychotherapist, lecturer and facilitator. I integrate mindfulness into many of my roles in life and I believe that a mindful family is definitely a happier family.

How to Read This Book

This book is not going to tell you how to parent or how to live together as a family. In fact, this book is not just about parenting. It is bigger than that. The word 'parenting' is centred on the parents, but a family includes everyone living in a home as well as everyone connected through either a biological or an assumed relationship. 'Parenting' also suggests a one-way action where the parent is the agent of action and the child is the beneficiary. While this may be valid till the child becomes a school-goer, it is important that we have a bigger picture in mind. Instead of 'parenting', think of it as co-creating a culture of mindfulness in our families.

In this book, we bring our experience of the various roles that we have played in a family setting. We want to present these ideas from the perspective of mindfulness practices and place them in your awareness. We invite you to experiment with them to see if they work for you, and then form your own blueprint for a way to live as a mindful family.

Part I looks into what mindfulness for families is and why we need it. Part II then offers 30 mindfulness activities that you can practise together with your children. Feel free to experiment with these activities, along with practising the 8 mindfulness practices introduced across the book, at your own pace.

As you make your way into this book, remember that the idea is not to strive to 'become' mindful, or to 'attain' a state of mindfulness. This expectation is an unhealthy one, as it plants the expectation in our mind to expect change. Instead, we recommend that you take a contemplative, non-striving approach to change. Change happens naturally when we simply practise mindfulness instead of striving for it.

We have written this book in a way that places information and intention in your awareness, and allows your mind to transform on its own. Your actions then arise from your very being. Please approach this book with the attitude that we cannot 'create' wisdom but only discover it through insights.

It is best that both parents are aligned when introducing mindfulness in the family. Single parents, co-parents and guardians can equally benefit from this book.

Let us now commence this inner journey.

Body Scan

Get in touch with your body and listen to its feedback. Train your attention to go inward and release emotions that may be stored in your body. Body Scan is practised by bringing attention to different parts of your body in turn. You could also use an audio practice file (available on the internet) to guide you.

1. Ensure you are in an environment where you have the least external distractions.

2. Lie down on an exercise/yoga mat or a flat surface that is comfortable and firm.

3. Close your eyes when you are ready.

4. Start your practice by mentally noticing the different parts of your body. First, bring your attention to your left leg, all the way down to your big toe and then the other toes. Slowly shift your awareness to the sole of your foot, ankle, calf muscle, and so on. Do this same process all the way to the top of your head.

6. Prepare a sequence based on the parts of your body, for example:

- Left leg
- Right leg
- Back of the torso
- Front of the torso
- Left arm
- Right arm
- Neck
- Face
- Back of the head

7. Notice each of these parts of your body for 30 seconds to 1 minute before moving on to the next section.

8. In order not to watch the time during your practice, wait till you have completed the entire body scan before you look at how much time you took altogether and then adjust your pace in your next practice accordingly.

Body Scan

With children, the Body Scan practice can be shortened to 10–15 minutes and is best guided by a parent. We have a recommended script below but feel free to adapt it as you feel necessary.

1. Lie down on an exercise/yoga mat or a flat surface that is comfortable and firm.

2, Let your legs and your arms relax and fall to the sides, and close your eyes.

3. Start by taking three deep breaths and noticing how that feels. Notice how your belly rises and falls as the air moves in and out of your body. Gently place your right hand on your chest and your left hand on your belly and feel them rise and fall with each in-breath and out-breath. Now place both hands by the side of the body and let them relax.

4. Now we are going to notice the other parts of your body. Let's start with your feet. Relax your feet and notice the sensations in your left foot. And now notice the right foot. It is also OK if you feel nothing at all.

5. For the next few minutes, let yourself just be. Pay attention to the best of your ability. You might feel the contact of the floor or the socks on your feet. When your attention drifts away, gently bring it back to your feet again.

6. Now move your attention to your lower legs, noticing the sensations there. Do they feel heavy, light, warm, cold, or something else?

7. Next, move your attention to your knees and relax them. Feel the top, back, and sides of your knees.

8. Now, letting go of your knees, move your attention to your thighs. Whatever you feel – or do not feel – is fine. Notice your thighs and let them relax. If your body feels restless, that is fine too. Notice the restlessness and then bring your attention to your thighs.

9. Now, gently move your attention to your belly. Notice how it always moves when you breathe, rising and falling. You might notice the touch of your clothing as you breathe. You might feel something on the inside too.

10. Letting go of your belly, shift your attention to your chest. Notice it rising and falling as you breathe. Whenever your attention goes away, gently bring your attention back to your chest, again and again.

11. Now, move your attention to your hands. They may be touching the bed, or the floor, or some part of your body. Relax them if you can. Notice the sensations in your left hand and then your right hand.

12. Now move your attention up to your arms. Just notice the sensations there, in your left arm and your right arm.

13. Letting go of your arms, gently move your attention to your back. How does it feel against the bed or the floor? Be curious.

14. Now move your attention to your neck and shoulders and relax them. Notice if there is any tension or tightness here. Relax your shoulders by moving them up and down. If your mind drifts away to some other thought, that's fine. Accept your mind as it is. Gently bring your attention back to your neck and shoulders.

15. Letting go of your neck and shoulders, now bring your attention to your face and head. Bring a gentle smile to your face and notice how that feels. What are the thoughts in your mind?

16. Now letting go of your face and head, relax your entire body and then spend a few minutes paying attention to your whole body.

17. As this practice ends, you may want to wiggle your toes and fingers. Now you may open your eyes and come back to a sitting position. Sit here for a minute before doing anything else.

CHAPTER 2

What is Mindfulness?

Mindfulness is one of the most rapidly growing sciences in the last 20 years. Every year, hundreds of research papers are being published across the globe from studies conducted by various universities and research centres. The findings show that mindfulness is impactful in clinical treatment, schools and the workplace. It has also been found to be very useful in parenting and love relationships.

The term 'mindfulness' was first introduced some 100 years ago by T.W. Rhys Davids. It has since become popularly associated with a specific aspect of Buddhist practice. However, it was in the Indic philosophies that mindfulness originally found prominence, going back some 2,000 years. Buddhism, Hinduism, Jainism and Yoga all have forms of mindfulness practices.

Research also suggests that mindfulness practices are found in Christianity, Islam and other religions as well.

While these practices were initially used in the religious sphere, in late 1970s a biologist and medical doctor by the name of Dr Jon Kabat-Zinn adapted them for secular audiences. His innovation came about from experiments with people suffering from chronic pain, stress, anxiety and illnesses at the University of Massachusetts. The experiments gave birth to Mindfulness-Based Stress Reduction (MBSR), the first evidence-based mindfulness programme.

Soon after, research on mindfulness started to grow, and the findings showed very positive results such as reduced stress, emotional regulation, performance enhancement, increase

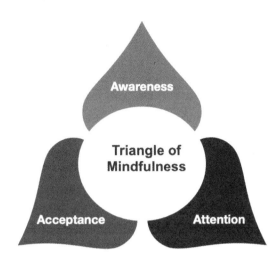

in positive mental states, reduced depression, enhanced resilience, etc. The success of MBSR led to other variants of mindfulness interventions such as Mindfulness-Based Cognitive Therapy (MBCT), Mindfulness-Based Leadership (MBL), Mindful Self-Compassion and Mindfulness-Based Wellbeing Enhancement (MBWE). These second-generation programmes not only alleviated clinical challenges but also sought to enhance personal performance and well-being.

This was how we approached mindfulness when we encountered it decades ago. With this approach, people who are not facing any specific challenges can also take advantage of mindfulness and enhance their quality of life.

Almost all secular mindfulness teachers and researchers use the works of Kabat-Zinn when it comes to defining and describing the concept of mindfulness. According to him, 'Mindfulness is awareness that arises through paying attention, on purpose, in the present moment, non-judgementally in the service of self-understanding and wisdom.'

This definition helps us to appreciate mindfulness through several key components: awareness, paying attention purposefully and in the present moment, and the concept of non-judgement. Kabat-Zinn also uses two other interesting words: self-understanding and wisdom. Secular mindfulness, then, is for the purpose of understanding the self and discovering wisdom. We will discuss more about these ideas in the pages to come.

Triangle of Mindfulness

We have found that mindfulness can be easily understood through the three A's: Awareness, Attention and Acceptance.

The first component, Awareness, is perhaps the single most important trait in mindfulness.

We consider awareness to be almost a synonym for mindfulness. Psychologists also call this trait 'metacognition', which means becoming aware of one's awareness.

The second aspect, Attention, can refer to concentration and focusing practices as well as what we eventually pay attention to as a disposition. In fact, all mindfulness practices involve attentional practices in one form or other. We pay attention to physical sensations, our breath, our thoughts.

Finally, Acceptance is the invitation of all experiences with a sense of accommodation during mindfulness practices and the ability to respond to life situations. We learn to accept discomfort, distractions, rumination and all of that without any kind of judgement.

In Chapter 6, we will delve deeper into these aspects.

State and Trait Mindfulness

Mindfulness is both a state and a trait. What do we mean by this? When we speak of mindfulness as a state, we are referring to mindfulness practices – the mental training practices that are interspersed throughout this book such as awareness of breath meditation, body scan, sitting meditation, coping breathing space, mindful eating, mindful walking, etc.

Mindfulness as a trait, on the other hand, refers to the effortless mastery of being anchored in the state of awareness naturally and at all times. This is when mindfulness becomes a habit, pervading your thoughts, emotions and behaviours.

Trait mindfulness is the outcome of consistent and sustained practice of informal and formal mindfulness practices. Research indicates that consistent daily practice leads to brain restructuring. Hence, there is a connection between mindfulness as a practice and mindfulness as a trait. One leads naturally to the other.

Trait mindfulness should not be mistaken as the state of 'enlightenment' proposed by some religious traditions. The trait mindfulness that we are referring to is a natural disposition of being anchored in awareness, attention and acceptance at all times. Research has shown that mindfulness gradually becomes a strong trait in people who have meditated for many years.

Trait mindfulness also shouldn't be mistaken as a permanent and irreversible state. Traits can be lost due to significant life events or a lack of sustained practice. That is why mindfulness practices should be a consistent feature in one's life.

Wisdom of Mindfulness

Let us now turn to the topic of wisdom, which was presented in the definition of mindfulness. A human being is called *Homo sapiens* for a reason. The term literally means 'wise man'. Carl Linnaeus, who came up with this name, maintained that the sole criterion that separates man from animals is the capacity to be noble.

In our opinion, this is indeed one of the most defining characteristics of a human being. Our capacity to process knowledge and experiences such that we learn to live it as wisdom is what makes us unique among all living creatures. We are not the strongest or the fastest, but we certainly have the capability to be wiser than all other creatures – although we may not always exercise that capacity readily.

Wisdom cannot be taught. It is not an explicit form of knowledge that can be gained via content, books, speeches or images. Instead, the wisdom that mindfulness creates comes from inside out.

Wisdom is the assimilated knowledge of the self, others and the world being connected. It is humanistic and responds in a way that promotes well-being and realises wholeness of all beings, not just oneself. With wisdom, we do not see ourselves as a master or ruler of the world in any way. Rather, we see ourselves as part of the world, an interconnected and interdependent systemic whole.

This is one of the reasons why we recommend that mindfulness be learned from another person, apart from reading about it from a book. While it is good to understand the structure, design and mechanics of a bicycle in learning to ride it, it is still best that we have a coach, such as our parents, to learn hands-on. We need both theory and practice.

Misconceptions

One of the biggest misconceptions about mindfulness is that it aims to put you in a non-thinking state. Such ideas are indeed promoted by other schools of contemplative philosophies, which may have their own merits, but not so in mindfulness.

When we mistakenly make it our objective to still the mind or to purge it of thoughts, we make thoughts the enemy. We start fighting with our thoughts. This is like being in a state of depression, where we have thoughts that may be unwholesome, and we keep ruminating on them. We try to reject these thoughts, only to make things worse.

It is similar to asking you not to think of an elephant, and then the elephant keeps appearing in your head. Every time you try to reject that elephant, it just keeps appearing. The same happens with anger, low mood, suicidal thoughts, unhappiness, etc.

Attempting to remove thoughts from your mind is similar to expecting a highway to be empty of cars. The highway is meant for cars and we shouldn't expect it to be otherwise.

In mindfulness, we learn to live with thoughts as they are. All mindfulness practices allow you to notice your thoughts without any illusions about them. By learning to pay attention to our breath, our bodily sensations as well as our thoughts and emotions, we learn to create a distance between the thoughts and ourselves. While a thought may come and go, your awareness remains a constant feature in spite of those thoughts. Enhancing the capacity to be aware then allows us to live with all types of difficult thoughts. This is one of the unique features of mindfulness, where we do not see thoughts as a problem.

There are many other misconceptions of mindfulness, such as mindfulness and yoga being the same, mindfulness reducing spirituality, and mindfulness being meant for older people, amongst many others. We won't go into each of them as not all are relevant to the topic of this book. We would like your own experience to speak for itself through this journey.

Benefits of Mindfulness

The research findings on the benefits of mindfulness are constantly building a strong case for mindfulness as a mainstream practice. Today, we have many research-validated scales and questionnaires that can be administered to measure the impact of mindfulness. Let us present some of these findings here.

Impact on the Brain

The first and foremost of the benefits is that our brains literally change structurally when practising mindfulness. The hippocampus, which is the seat of learning and memory, has been found to become thicker with mindfulness practices. This happened with just 8 weeks of mindfulness practices. The amygdala – which is responsible for the fight, flight and freeze reactions – was also found to have its brain cell volume reduce. This has a significant impact on the reduction of anxiety, fear and stress.

Mindfulness practitioners with over 20 years of practice have been found to have a better-preserved brain as they aged, and the impact was pervasive in the brain. Mind wandering and unhappiness related to the Default Mode Network of the brain were also found to be positively impacted with mindfulness practices.

In our experience with people we have taught over the years, many report that their concentration abilities and attentional capabilities improved within two weeks of practice. And research findings support this as well.

We would like you to now imagine if you could relate better with your children and loved ones as you age with a healthier brain, better memory, less reactivity and happier self. This is one of the value propositions of mindfulness.

Mental and Physical Health

When faced with difficult situations in our daily affairs, we often react impulsively, or let our emotions derail us. Research shows that mindfulness practices reduce this 'reactivity', helping us to respond in more considered ways. Over time, our emotional regulation abilities become strengthened, allowing us to choose the right action in any given situation.

Mindfulness also helps with increasing positive states of mind such as compassion, empathy, respect and curiosity. It is motivating for us to pay attention to them in our daily living for enhanced well-being.

Given that the world is rapidly changing and increasingly unpredictable, resilience is more important than ever. We have found mindfulness practitioners to be highly resilient to challenging and volatile situations. Such skills can help both adults and children better deal with unpredictable environments.

Other psychological results of mindfulness are the ability to be content, giving objective attention to experiences, acceptance of the body, increased optimism and self-compassion.

Researchers have found that mindfulness can enhance mastery over the body, relieve stress, lower blood pressure, improve sleep and lower weight, amongst other health benefits. It also facilitates recovery from chronic or potentially terminal illness, and has shown positive results in reducing depression, bipolar disorder, anxiety disorder and eating disorders.

A longitudinal study of female college students in 2011 found that higher levels of trait mindfulness were linked to better physical health. The students experienced better quality of sleep and had healthier eating habits. Another study found that mindfulness practitioners had better cardiovascular and psychological health. In 2019, researchers found that mindfulness improved pain management amongst chronic patients.

In 2012, a researcher from the University of Exeter found that mindfulness improved the well-being of children and young people. This included reduction in anxiety, stress and reactivity, and concurrently, improvement in their self-esteem, sleep quality, calmness and relaxation. The children learned to self-regulate and improve both their self-awareness and social awareness.

Relationships

The primary focus of this book is the family, which involves relationships such as parent-child, siblings, parent-grandparent, spouses, child-grandparent, etc. It is inevitable that conflicts occasionally arise as a result of these relational dynamics. Sometimes these conflicts can leave a deep scar that is hard to repair.

In the deepest of our hearts, what we look for in relationships is wholesomeness, which contributes to everyone's well-being. However, reality doesn't always meet our expectations. This gap between expectations and outcomes may create conflicts.

Mindfulness has been found to have a significant positive impact on relationships by increasing the quality of our relationships and equipping us to handle any conflicts that arise with wisdom. Furthermore, being attentive and centred in the present moment help us build intimacy and closeness because we start

noticing the little changes that our minds usually fail to catch.

Finally, compassion, empathy and kindness help us to resolve conflicts much more effectively rather than resorting to anger, impulse or violence. In 2018, researchers looked at three studies on the impact of mindfulness and partner-acceptance and found that trait mindfulness led to participants becoming more accepting of their partner's shortcomings, which ultimately led to greater relationship satisfaction.

Benefits for Children

There is a steadily growing body of evidence on the benefits of mindfulness in children. In our study of the latest research, we reviewed more than 20 papers across eight countries and found very interesting results.

Our study revealed that 76% of the research papers reported that mindfulness had a significant impact on Self-Management, one of the five key competencies in the Social Emotional Learning (SEL) framework. The SEL is being adopted across the globe with regard to measuring the impact of learning in schools. About 25% of the papers found an impact on the other four competencies – Self-Awareness, Social Awareness, Relationship Skills and Responsible Decision-making.

In another study, we found the following benefits of mindfulness practices for school-going children and teens:

- Supports readiness to learn
- Promotes academic performance
- Strengthens attention
- Reduces anxiety before examinations, assessments and tests
- Promotes self-reflection and self-calming
- Improves classroom participation by supporting impulse control
- Fosters pro-social behaviours and healthy relationships
- Supports holistic well-being

A research study in 2018 in England found that young people enjoyed mindfulness practices and used the skills they learned to cope with stressful situations.

Among tertiary students, research that we conducted over four years revealed that mindfulness reduces stress levels, increases happiness levels and enhances self-awareness.

Given that the effects of mindfulness on school-going children are highly consistent, we can safely say that mindfulness is an invaluable new skill to be developed in children.

In the last five years, we have trained thousands of students and teachers. Our work led us to think: What if we brought mindfulness into the homes of children and included the parents in mindfulness practices, so that the whole family could benefit from it together?

Parents are the ones who have a wholehearted interest in the well-being of their children. In schools, mindfulness programmes are inevitably dependent on the school strategy and priorities within their curriculum. Hence, bringing mindfulness into the family can make a greater, more far-reaching and sustainable impact.

Through a concerted effort to sustain mindfulness practices in the home, parents can make it a home culture. Practising mindfulness then enhances the quality of the parent-child time together.

And ultimately, through that, we may discover our true *Homo sapiens* nature: the capacity to be wise. In the next chapter, we will explore more about ourselves as simple human beings.

Awareness of Breath

The purpose of this practice is to learn to simply be with your breath and yourself without judgement, to be in a calm, non-judging awareness, allowing your thoughts and feelings to come and go without getting caught up in them. You may also take advantage of one of the many audio practice files available on the internet to guide you.

1. Adopt a comfortable sitting posture which keeps your back upright and relaxed. You can sit on the ground or on a chair.

2. Close your eyes, if you like.

3. Bring your attention to your breathing, either by observing the breath at your nostrils or the rise and fall of your chest and abdomen.

4. Whenever your thoughts distract you, simply notice them, and then gently but firmly bring your attention back to your breathing.

5. Bring curiosity to your practice. Is your breath fast or slow? Is it deep or shallow? It is natural for thoughts to enter into your awareness, and for your attention to follow them. No matter how many times this happens, gently bring your attention back to your breathing. Your breath is always with you. Use your breath to anchor yourself.

6. As the meditation ends, give yourself credit for having spent this time in a state of being.

Awareness of Breath

With children, this practice can be shortened to 5 minutes. We have a recommended script below for you to guide your child with, but feel free to adapt it as required. Ensure that your child is seated on the floor with a cushion or on a comfortable chair.

1. Let us begin the practice by sitting comfortably. Gently close your eyes so that you are not distracted by the moving objects around us.

2. Breathe as you normally would without changing the pace of your in-breath and out-breath. Bring your attention to the physical sensation of each in-breath and out-breath. You can also notice the rising and falling of your belly or your chest.

3. The mind is always busy. It may drift away from the breath. That is normal and okay, because that is what minds do. Just accept that and then gently bring your attention back to your breath.

4. Breathe in and breathe out. Breathe in and breathe out. The breath is always with us in the present time. Notice every single breath that goes into your body and every single breath that leaves the body.

5. Be curious about your breath:

- Is it fast or slow?
- Is it cool or warm?
- Which part of your body expands and contracts as you breathe?

6. When your mind wanders, gently bring it back to noticing your breathing. Thoughts will be there when you are practising mindfulness. And this is fine. Just return to the breath, again and again.

7. Notice every single inhalation and exhalation. Your breath is always with you. Focus on your breath.

Breathe in. Breathe out.
Breathe in. Breathe out.
Breathe in. Breathe out.
Breathe in. Breathe out.
Breathe in. Breathe out.

8. When you are ready, gently open your eyes.

CHAPTER 3

Who Am I?

In order for us to appreciate the value and intention of mindfulness in families, we need to first recognise certain fundamental truths about our lives as human beings. These are primarily the biological and relational aspects of our development. And there is a connection between these aspects of our lives.

Biological and Psychosocial Stages

Broadly, as human beings, we undergo the following stages of life:

Child → Adult → Senior

Starting with being born, childhood is a stage of rapid physical growth. Around the age of 12 years, we transit into adolescence, and around the age of 20 or so, we glide into adulthood. By the age of about 65 years, we become seniors.

Childhood is the stage where our mental, emotional and social dimensions are formed. These become the foundation on which our adult life and senior life are built and developed. Psychologists view this childhood stage as significantly contributing to the formation of personality. Thus what we sow during this period sprouts, grows and manifests through our adulthood and senior years.

Mental development takes place both passively and actively. In passive learning, the child exhibits curiosity and puts almost everything in its mouth after touching and feeling it. Active learning, on the other hand, takes place when elders teach and train the child. Moral foundations and knowledge about the external world come through this form of learning.

A child's psychosocial development can affect their personality. Until the age of about 18

months, a child is dependent on her parents to provide consistent care, support, love, predictability and stability. When this is provided, the child grows up to feel secure and trusts other adults. When it is missing, the child becomes distrustful and suspicious of people around and feels insecure.

Even in adolescence, there is a dependence on parents or adults for guidance. This is a stage when children start to explore their values, goals in life, sexual identity, body image and various roles, amongst other things. When adolescents do not fully explore this stage or find answers to their questions about themselves, they can experience role confusion instead of forming a clear self-identity.

As adults, our physical growth halts, except for perhaps changes in our weight primarily influenced by lifestyle choices or sometimes health issues. This is also the stage where we explore love relationships, with success resulting in a secure and committed relationship. Avoidance of intimacy, on the other hand, leads to isolation and loneliness.

Around the age of 40, we pay more attention to doing things that are part of a bigger picture, which give us a greater sense of accomplishment. These include having and raising children, having a job, being productive in our work, contributing to society. The reverse of this is being stagnant in one's development and feeling disconnected from the world.

As we enter our senior stage, our body slowly loses its moisture and muscle. We start looking smaller and perhaps even frail. Some of our bodily functions may also get impacted. From the perspective of psychosocial development, some of us may look back on our life and feel that we have contributed to ourselves, our families and society at large. Or we may experience despair if we feel guilt and regret over our past.

Now that we have seen what happens to our biological self and psychosocial self, let's explore the development of our roles and relationships across the span of our lives.

Relational Development

Relational development is connected to our identities, many of which are connected to our biological stage in life. Here is an example of the stages of development and the roles we play during each one:

Stage	Roles
Child	Son/Daughter Student Citizen
Adult	Son/Daughter Lover Spouse Parent Employee/Employer Citizen
Senior	Son/Daughter Spouse Parent Grandparent Citizen

In any relationship, there is a second person needed for the relationship to exist. For example, the role of a daughter is in reference to a parent, and they are mutually dependent. So is a spousal relationship, where the relationship depends on both partners. When the husband dies, the role of the wife gets renamed, as widowhood.

As we can see, some relationships continue on and some get terminated at some point. Some relationships get replaced, like when the lover becomes a spouse. Some roles were given to us, for example the role of son/daughter. We did not get to choose our parents. And there are no terms like ex-son or ex-mother. On the other hand, roles like that of a spouse are something we choose, and a spouse can become an ex-spouse.

Each relationship creates a unique set of responsibilities:

Roles → Relationships → Responsibilities

For example, the role of the mother is connected to the parent-child relationship. And there are responsibilities for the mother to ensure that the parent-child relationship is wholesome and that the parent provides for the child in the early years of development. Responsibilities can be legitimised by religious and spiritual beliefs as well.

Mindful Families

A family is broadly defined as a group of people sharing common ancestors. For the purpose of this book, however, we focus on the relationship between parents and their children. In any family setup, it is the people who play the role of parents who take on the responsibility for co-creating a mindful family.

What does a mindful family look like? It is one that provides a supportive environment founded on compassion, empathy and kindness to one other. Problems or challenges become opportunities for the family members to support one another. All the members the family, especially the parents, cultivate self-awareness so that they can better understand themselves before they try to understand others.

At this juncture, you may feel that co-creating a mindful family could be an additional burden to your role, given that parenting is already tough. If so, I would like you to see mindfulness as the grease that keeps the moving parts in your family from not creating friction. Thus your parenting efforts will become less stressful and more meaningful.

A 2016 research study, where some 300 parents were trained in mindfulness, found an increase in dispositional mindfulness and self-compassion. In a 2018 study, parents who practised mindfulness were found to parent more positively. They also reported better parent-child relationships and positive changes in aggression in the youths. This aligns with the findings of a study of mindful parenting programmes over a 17-year period, which showed that mindful parents were more aware of the emotions of their 10-to-14-year-old children. In yet another research, it was found that children whose mothers were mindful were more likely to exhibit sharing behaviour and pro-social behaviour.

Bringing mindfulness into the family is thus not only possible but also highly rewarding.

Parenting as the Pivotal role

We believe that parenting is a labour of love. Children are born of love, sustained by their parents' love, and continue to share that love with others as well as sharing it with their children when they become parents. It is on the foundation of love that parenting happens, whether consciously or unconsciously.

When a child grows up in a loving home, where parents are available during distress and provide protection and comfort, the child grows up feeling secure and is able to form intimate and lasting relationships in future. She is confident, has higher self-esteem and is a positive contributor to society.

Research by psychologists John Bowlby and Mary Ainsworth on the attachment between a parent and child reinforces the need to have a strong and secure bond with your children. Your love for your children, when consciously manifested, becomes a tool for promoting well-being in your family.

Let us now explore parenting from multiple perspectives.

As human beings, we share four traits with animals: sleep, fear, procreative instincts and food. It is parenting that makes children discover that they are *Homo sapiens* who are more sophisticated than the sum of these four traits. Parenting is an invitation to the child to discover wholeness and wholesomeness. We use the term 'invitation' because at times this invitation may not be accepted by some children, through no fault of the parents.

We have seen children ending up leading unwholesome lives in spite of having wise parents, amazing friends and having attended the best of educational institutions. I (Kathir) had a high school friend who was the best in my cohort for four straight years, a very intelligent guy who shunned my company because he considered me and my friends to be too playful. He was the boy who never gave his teachers any problems. But by the time he went into National Service (Singapore's two-year compulsory conscription into the military for males), he had become a different person. He was a heavy smoker and an alcoholic. This is an exception, but it can happen to anyone.

There are also many forces, known and unknown, influencing the outcome of your parenting which you are not in control of.

From birth, children exhibit different temperaments, and these temperaments shape their growth. So while parents have a significant impact on the child's growth, it is not absolute. In spite of giving our best, children may still become someone other that what we expect them to be. Hence, as parents your responsibilities are only to give your best and to be self-compassionate and other-compassionate when things turn out otherwise.

The fact that every parent was once a child is perhaps the most important thing that we need to acknowledge. Our own experience as children influences our beliefs about parenting. If we deem that our parents were bad people or not good enough as parents, we strive to be better parents. If we deem them to be awesome, we aim to follow in their footsteps.

Of course, it is highly possible that the parents do their level best in their parenting and yet their child becomes a less than wholesome parent. When we dig deep into our memories of when we were a child, it is obvious that our earliest behaviour was to make everything in our life as comfortable and enjoyable as possible. We wanted toys, friends, gadgets, tasty food, snacks and permissive parents too.

We wanted to be happy. But are you happy right now?

We wanted to do whatever came to our mind. Are you doing whatever you feel like doing right now?

We had dreams of being a singer, dancer, artist and many other dreams. Are you fulfilling those dreams?

If you have not had a happy life, you could possibly deem that everyone's life is as miserable as yours, or you might envy the lives of others and make yourself more miserable. These assumptions can influence your parenting style and thus you may put in extra effort to make your child's life more comfortable and enjoyable. It is a type of compensating behaviour where we consciously or unconsciously cover up feelings of inadequacy through gratification in other areas of life (e.g. our career) or becoming a better parent than our own parents. We need to be aware of these assumptions we make as a result of our childhood experiences.

It is clear that as parents we want our children to do well in their lives. All beings, humans and animals alike, are instinctively programmed to make sacrifices for their children. As parents you may be sacrificing your comforts, time, jobs and even happiness for the sake of your children. We believe that both parents and children should do well in their lives. You should not forsake your well-being in the process of achieving wellness and happiness for your children.

We are not proposing that you should not work hard to give your children the best. Rather, what is important is giving your children wholesome life experiences which can take place even in a remote village or in an urban city state like Singapore. It is what is in your mind that determines the outcomes and not what you create in the external world.

The Purpose of Parenthood

There are countless reasons why you became a parent. It could have been by choice or by accident. It could have been influenced by your religious beliefs or perhaps you always wanted to start a family or you just found babies adorable. It is also possible that it was due to the boredom of couplehood, or social and family pressures, or the fear of loneliness in your senior years.

Regardless of the reason, you are now a parent in the present moment. You have two choices. One is to let it be and do as you want. The other is to find your purpose as a parent. Between the two, the mindful way is to define your purpose. Accept the past and make a conscious decision to define your purpose as a parent.

Take five minutes at this juncture and write down in the space below your parenting purpose statement. We are giving you four guiding criteria that your statement should satisfy:

1. Wholesome: The statement must be aimed at the well-being of the world, society, family and oneself (parent and child).

2. Positive: It should be written with positive words such 'I want my child to understand happiness' as opposed to 'I don't want my child to be unhappy'.

3. Exciting: It should excite and motivate you as a parent.

4. Mindful: It should implicitly raise self-awareness in your child and yourself.

An example of a purpose statement:

'I want my family to be of service to each other, to grow together by understanding each other, to take care of each other's and the planet's well-being.'

Your purpose statement:

Growing Up as Children

We watch children grow and develop through biological as well as cultural and environmental influences. From sleeping two-thirds of the day and crying for everything needed as an infant, to learning to walk and grabbing things that they desire and asking for what they need, they start to express more and more emotions, their psychomotor and cognitive skills improve, and parents celebrate each of these great milestones.

Let us now look at the child's life from their perspective. Children learn much about life through the pain-pleasure continuum. In infants, pain and discomfort are often associated with crying. Infants cry during birth, when hungry or in discomfort. They also cry when they see a stranger or happen to experience something they do not like. Children naturally avoid painful experiences.

Pleasure is often expressed by infants with smiles and laughter. Tickling them or giving them what they want makes them smile and laugh. Familiar faces and voices or even the smells of loved ones elicit the same reactions.

These two types of experience form the bedrock of their emotional growth and their ability to be resilient. Our biological experiences with pain and pleasure are not different from animals. Animals, too, persistently avoid pain and seek pleasure.

However, as human beings, we need to take another step to enable a capacity that we possess: the wisdom of processing our experiences. This is usually learned through parenting, as we slowly allow children to process pain and pleasure in a way that allows them to grow with wisdom.

This usually happens after the age of four or five for most children, when they know what objects and experiences provide pleasure or pain and how to manage some of these experiences by either avoiding or seeking them. Parents can then start helping their child understand pain and pleasure rather than just reacting to them.

The biggest misconception that a child learns in the first four years of her life is to associate pain with unhappiness and pleasure with happiness. This association is usually carried right through to adulthood and clouds our appreciation of what is good and what is not. This spells challenges for many children when they become adults.

The unwholesome outcome that happens is 'avoiding' pain and 'seeking' pleasure. This avoidance or seeking can eventually manifest in bigger life problems. As adults we would then choose what is acceptable based on this criterion. Any experience that does not conform to this criterion would be deemed as unacceptable. On the other hand, seeking pleasure would then become an eternal pursuit.

The above experiences create a natural belief that pain leads to unhappiness and therefore it is wrong, while pleasure leads to happiness and is therefore right.

Pain = Unhappiness → Right

Pleasure = Happiness → Wrong

Indeed, the world's foremost problems can be traced back to these two equations. Excessive consumption has led to the creation of too much waste, which has become a global problem. We are losing trees, metal ores and oil due to this as well. We start to take more from the planet (for pleasure) rather than making an effort to contribute (through effort, i.e. pain) towards the growth of the planet.

This leads us to the purpose of parenting. We need to bring a wise and wholesome way of breaking down the instinctual equations that we have formed by the time our child reaches the age of four.

Firstly, let us debunk the belief that painful experiences lead to unhappiness while pleasurable experiences make us happy. There are many situations in your life where painful experiences have been happy moments, such as giving birth to a new life, helping someone in need or exercising hard to improve your health. There are also pleasurable experiences such as substance abuse and alcoholic addictions that bring temporary happiness in the moment but unhappiness in the long term. Therefore, equating experiences with

happiness or unhappiness and thereby concluding that they are right or wrong is completely illusory.

What we need is a yardstick to accurately examine our experiences to see if they are conducive to our well-being. We propose that the most important question you should pose to yourself when faced with any potential experience is:

Is this wholesome?

Wholesomeness is defined by the Collins Dictionary as something that 'is likely to have a positive influence on people's behaviour or mental state'. This is an objective question and it helps us to identify what is right.

This is a very important inquiry that you as a parent can use to understand if something is beneficial to your child. Ask yourself if it is going to be a wholesome experience. In time, your child will be able to apply the same yardstick, to discern what is right or wrong.

At this point, some of you may be thinking that fun and joyful things are not wholesome. But this is not true. It is natural and human to seek out fun and joy and hence we need to satisfy that as well. But too much of it becomes unwholesome.

Process and Outcomes are Both Important

There is also an erroneous belief that in parenting the process is more important than the outcome. While there is an ounce of truth in this, we need to add another component into this overly simplistic dictum. Between the process of parenting and the outcomes of parenting, there is the goal of parenting.

Purpose → Goals → Process → Outcomes

The process of parenting has a clear purpose. The purpose you identified for yourself earlier is the one that helps you to identify the many goals that you have. For example, for the purpose statement below, you could come up with many goals.

Purpose:

'I want my family to be of service to each other, to grow together by understanding each other, to take care of each other's and the planet's well-being.'

Goals:

- To raise kind, empathetic children
- To have strong and healthy children
- To create good human beings
- To nurture supportive sibling relationships
- To eat healthy food, and so on

While we set goals for the purpose that we have identified, the process of parenting helps you to achieve these goals. However, there are many slips between the cup and your lips. What you set as a goal for yourself may not materialise in the way you expected. These are the outcomes. In mindful families, we learn to accept these outcomes regardless of what they may be. We will discuss more about the quality of acceptance a little later in the book.

Nevertheless, while we accept these outcomes, we may sometimes still need to do something so that we can course-correct or even possibly ditch some goals. We can train our minds to do this diligently and conscientiously.

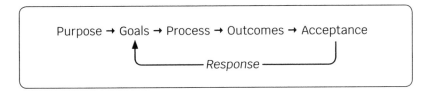

The Need for Mindful Children

The goal of mindfulness for the family is to inspire mindful parents, mindful children and a wholesome relationship between the two.

Mindful children are children who are grounded in the present moment with a future focus. They develop themselves to be self-aware, responsible and have a keen sense of paying attention. They embody compassion, empathy and kindness. These traits transform them to be able to constantly better themselves in academics and life skills because they see themselves as a 'work in progress'. These attitudes are carried right through to adulthood, where they become mature human beings.

Mindfulness also helps children with reducing active and passive aggression. Parents often complain that one of the biggest challenges in their children is aggression as a reaction to unfavourable situations, which manifests in throwing tantrums, whining and back-talking. This happens because children find it difficult to accept situations and experiences. It is also contributed to by their belief that what is right has to be pleasurable. Another reason for this behaviour could be the lack of compassion for others and for themselves.

Children face many unprecedented challenges in the world today. There are some as young as five who experience depression and anxiety. School-going children report being bullied and having relationship issues. Academic performance and expectations from both teachers and parents subject them to stress and emotional strain. Family problems such as lack of finances or violence can also impact children greatly. With technology, children are at risk of being preyed on by cyberstalkers and cyberbullies. They are also vulnerable to fake news when they do not have the ability to discern between real and fake.

An unstable home makes these problems worse. We have also encountered children who were psychologically abused. The parents were themselves going through difficult times or experiencing stress, and they unconsciously became aggressive towards their children by shouting at them or using hurtful words and actions. These aggressive behaviours create a relationship of 'insecure attachment', as defined by Bowlby and Ainsworth, which in turn leads to challenges when these children become adults.

Teenage suicide is on the rise. This is related to another challenge in our modern society, where mental health is declining, and socio-emotional resilience weakening. Teen pregnancies and underage sex are also on the rise and becoming common. Another challenge among teens is substance abuse. While most of them know that these are unwholesome behaviours, they are unable to resist the temptation, because the stress and need have become overwhelming. This tells us that our minds tend to react to stimuli without taking a pause. The ability to pause at any given time to consider the wholesomeness of an action is a vital skill to develop in our children.

You and your children might be facing one or more of these challenges. We cannot blame technology or other environmental factors for these problems entirely. What we have in our power to do is to anticipate these challenges and prepare our children to face them with wisdom.

We do that by becoming more mindful as a family. The burden of change does not solely rest on the shoulders of parents, but also on the children, although it is the former who lead these efforts. The change has to happen together as a family. And this will only happen with self-awareness, other-awareness, acceptance, compassion and love.

Mindful Eating

This practice can be done together with your child. The purpose of Mindful Eating is to help bring our minds to the present moment, to what is right in front of us, and thus reduce autopilot behaviours.

1. Seeing: Look at your food. Take time to really focus on it with care and full attention. Look at it as if this is the first time you are seeing it. Look at the container, arrangement, colours, layers, smoothness and variety.

2. Holding and touching: Take one spoonful or a piece of the food. Is it heavy and dense? Or light and fluffy? Is it smooth, rough or slimy? What else do you notice?

3. Smelling: Bring the food closer to your nose. With each inhalation, take in the smell. Is it fragrant? What does it smell like? Does it trigger any memories?

4. Entering the mouth: Place the food in your mouth but don't start chewing. Notice how it gets into your mouth in the first place. Focus on the sensations.

5. Tasting: Take one bite and observe what happens. Notice the juice, flavour and sensations. Is it bitter, sweet, sour or salty? What is unique about the taste? Take another bite.

6. Hearing: As you chew, notice the sounds. What do you hear? Is the food loud and crunchy?

7. Swallowing: After sufficient chewing, swallow the mouthful of food, and notice the sensations as you do so.

8. Take your next bite, and again, chew as slowly as you can, taking your time to explore all the sensations at your own pace.

CHAPTER 4

Why Mindful Parenting?

The challenges that parents face today come from both within and without. However, between the two, it is what is happening inside of you that is of interest to us when it comes to mindfulness.

It is not that we should turn a blind eye to what is happening outside us, which is the external environment and the forces that govern it. Rather, in mindfulness, we are anchored in the internal workings of the mind that take place as a result of our interaction with the external environment. The external world is perceived and processed by the internal world – the mind. Hence, mindfulness has an inside-out orientation in contrast to an outside-in experience, which we have limited control over.

It is like the weather, which we have limited control over, but we can make choices to overcome its challenges, for example by staying at home during a blizzard, or using an umbrella in rain, or wearing lighter clothes when it is blazing hot. We are unable to change the environment, but we can certainly adapt to it.

Let us examine some of the many challenges that parents experience within.

The Knower-Doer Conflict

The knower-doer conflict is perhaps a difficult experience for many. Parents tell and remind themselves often not to get angry with their children and yet they become angry and lash out at their children, only to regret the behaviour later.

Or perhaps you made an intention to take your children to the park but you forgot about it when other urgent matters cropped up and took your mind space, or you were simply distracted by your other role demands. From the children's standpoint, this is a broken promise. They do not understand your constraints or the multiple hats that you wear. They see you only as their parent.

Therefore, there could be a big gap between our intentions and the reality of life. This informs us that our minds can hold us hostage. This tendency can pervade other parts of our lives too, not just in our role as a parent. We know what we need to do but we do otherwise. This may even become a habit after a while and we pass these traits to our children unconsciously. This is the knower-doer conflict that everyone goes through.

The Autopilot

The autopilot is another tendency we possess in our brain. It is a function of the mind which propels us to act without thinking twice and without being aware of the present moment. Daniel Kahneman describes this thinking process as System 1, whereby we process information really fast, unconsciously and automatically.

A simple example of this behaviour could be habitually washing your face in the morning and then asking yourself if you have washed your face. It could also be the unconscious brushing of your teeth. We do not notice the contact of the toothbrush bristles on our teeth and gums when we are brushing our teeth, we are thinking of something else. Or we rush through our meals without tasting.

The impact of this is that we are not noticing that parenting is a 24/7 affair in a family. We may become unconscious about our thoughts, emotions, feelings and behaviours while we are with our families. This becomes a blind spot and even our unwholesome behaviours go under the radar. However, your children notice it and learn from it.

Psychologists identify a type of cognitive bias called 'bias blind spot', where we are unable to detect biases in ourselves but able to detect them in others. This has a detrimental impact on our judgements and behaviours.

For example, you may believe that you made an objective decision about the school your child should go to while you believe your friend was just being prejudiced in choosing her alma mater for her child. Perhaps both of you were objective or both of you were prejudiced? The bias blind spot is just one of the many cognitive biases that influence our thinking.

Unconscious Living

Living mindlessly or unconsciously is another phenomenon that may be a challenge for all of us. We are like passersby in our own lives. The impact of this can be profound, especially when we reach our senior years and ask ourselves: How did we get here?

What do you look forward to when you wake up in the morning? What is your purpose?

Our goals get replaced one by one as we journey through life. When we were young, it was toys that we wanted. And then it got replaced by friends and then a little later, the boyfriend or the girlfriend. And then your work and your spouse took your attention. And then when a child arrived, it became a new world, and then much later, grandchildren consume our attention. This goes on and on. There is no end to the roles we play and how our attention gets pulled in multiple directions. When our purpose keeps changing too frequently, then our life becomes purposeless.

The mindful way of living consciously would have all of your goals aligned with your purpose. We then start living our life instead of looking for a purpose.

A useful illustration for this would be a wheel. Like the way the spokes are connected to the hub, living mindfully means having all your goals connected to your purpose. It is in the hub where you live mindfully, where

your purpose is clear. Living in the present moment, anchored in your purpose, is what we call mindful living.

Soft Parenting

The other challenge is that parents often assume that mindful parenting is soft parenting, which is characterised by being permissive. Parents mollycoddle their children when soft parenting is the preferred style of parenting. This happens especially when parents feel guilty for not giving, doing, or spending enough time with their children.

Being permissive with children has to do with your beliefs. It could happen when parents are mostly absent from the child's life or with busy working parents. Parents tend to overcompensate for the lost time.

How does this manifest? Well, it could be by unconsciously allowing the child to form unwholesome beliefs or habits, such as by not correcting the child when he does something wrong. Soft parenting contributes to the 'snowflake generation', where children are unable to accept negative feedback and become less resilient.

Mindful parenting is not soft parenting but rather purposeful and intentional parenting.

Possibility of Narcissism

We once saw a parent doing something very interesting. Her toddler was playing with a bunch of kids. The toddler accidentally hit a wall and fell while chasing his friends. The mother immediately hit the wall with her bare hands as if the wall had done something to make her child fall. Imagine what the toddler takes away from this experience. He learns that failures are caused by others while successes are all of his own effort.

This brings another challenge for parents, which is the unconscious promotion of narcissism in children. Narcissism can actually make children feel less empathetic towards others and they tend to see things in a way that empowers their ego. It makes them feel superior to others, worthy of admiration. This can lead to bullying behvaiours as well. Our responses to children potentially reinforce their growing narcissism.

Personality Traits

Your personality plays a part in creating challenges for yourself. Some of you may have heard of or even completed a personality profiling assessment such as the MBTI, DISC or Emergenetics. Your personality can be a barrier between you and a person having another personality type, or perhaps complement it. This applies to your children, too.

If you happen to be someone who is easily stressed, this could create tension with your child. And if your child happens to have an avoidant personality, then these issues may create a distance between the two of you and possibly become a challenge in their teen and adult years.

Personality traits are difficult to change, though not impossible. Hence what is needed is to understand each other's style and come to a compromise and focus on whether the outcome is wholesome. For example, your child may feel that exercising in the outdoors is what works for her but you may prefer to be on a treadmill. There is no right or wrong in each of your preferences. Both of them can equally lead to the same outcome of being healthy.

Parenting Style

This leads to another challenge, which is using the same style of parenting from infanthood right into the teenage years. As discussed earlier, a child's needs change as he matures. Your parenting style needs to change accordingly.

Stopping a 2-year-old child in his tracks when he is trying to grab a hornet would be considered an appropriate approach to parenting. However, you cannot use that same style when you want stop your teenage daughter from doing something rash such as drink-driving. Your parenting style must adapt to the maturity of the child. Your child who is going to a new school, having a crush and realising their independence would need a different response.

In general, more conversations and looser boundaries (yes, there are still boundaries for them) are required as they grow older and become teenagers. Further down the road, you may need to renegotiate your parenting style when they become adults and parents themselves.

Me Time

Parents also find it very difficult to find enough time for themselves. We have seen many families where one of the parents makes the choice to be a stay-at-home parent while the other works, especially in the early years of the child's life. This tells us that parents see the value of time with their children as an effective ingredient in the process of parenting.

But certainly, with both parents working, parents may feel that balancing work demands and parenting demands takes its toll. It puts a strain on the limited number of hours available in a day, resulting in them not having time for themselves.

Parents often sacrifice their self-care, me-time and even couple time for the sake of time with their children. Making quality time for oneself becomes a rarity. As time goes on, this becomes a norm, where the parents' goals become a lower priority than the time with their children. This may lead to another set of problems, such as burnout, relationship strain between spouses and poor health, amongst others.

Children then perpetuate this cycle of what we call façade parenting, where parents don a happy and cheerful face in front of their children while feeling miserable or conflicted inside. As much as you may think that children do not notice, the opposite is true. They are able to notice your regular frustrated responses to other members of the family.

In fact, parenting narratives should include both the good and the bad, the beautiful and the ugly moments. It is about accepting and embracing every part of ourselves and willing to be vulnerable in front of our children without the need to be seen as a super-parent as that is an impossible pair of shoes to fill. When we can fully accept ourselves, so can our children.

Separation and Distance

If you happen to be a single parent – whether through separation, divorce, distance, widowhood or the absence of your spouse – then this poses challenges of its own.

A separation or divorce may bring about co-parenting challenges. Devoting time for each of the parents can sometimes be difficult, especially if you do not approve of the association of your child with your ex-spouse. Feelings such as resentment and anger may leak out unconsciously through your behaviour.

That said, sometimes separation or divorce leads to better well-being for the parents and children involved. A study in 2005 found that unhappily married couples had lower levels of happiness and life satisfaction compared to couples who were divorced and remarried.

If the other parent happens to be absent due to an overseas job or long working hours, you are holding the fort at home with singular responsibility. The parent who is frequently away spends minimal time with the child, and may not be able to relate well with the child. You end up compensating for that lost time and contact – or sometimes even having to justify it.

If the absence is due to the death of a parent, grief may manifest in the life of the child and the living parent. I (Kathir) went through such an experience when I lost my father at the age of 13. I was extremely close to him. When he passed on, I was badly affected, and seeing my mother being emotional most of the time made it much tougher. We must never underestimate the impact of losing a parent, especially if the child had a memorable relationship with them.

Dealing with all of the above is not easy for any parent or child. In a study of 6,500 respondents in Russia over a 5-year period, researchers found that stable marital status led to greater happiness. This and many other research studies lead us to believe that divorce, separation and the death of a spouse may generally negatively impact a parent's happiness and thus the child's well-being.

Mental Health

Although most research shows that parents are happier than non-parents, there is also evidence that being a parent can have a negative effect on one's mental health.

A 2019 study in the United States found that the impact depends on the age of the youngest child. Parents with children under 13 reported having more symptoms of anxiety and less life satisfaction. With parents of children aged 13–17, anxiety and less life satisfaction continued on, with an additional challenge of experiencing less frequent positive emotions. With slightly older children, parents were even found to have symptoms of depression. These issues were alleviated in parents with children over 30. Another research in 2006 found that satisfaction in marriage decreased when children were born and improved only after the children left home.

As much as parents report being happier when they have children, we can see that happiness and poor health are not mutually exclusive. You can be happy but in poor health if the responsibilities of parenting become your top priority without any outlet for yourself.

Work-Life Balance

Balancing work and parenthood is another challenge, particularly with dual-income families. Caring for an infant while juggling job demands can certainly create a recipe for regret, guilt and even self-judgement if not managed well.

In a 2011 German research study, it was found that parenthood reduced mothers' work hours and adversely affected their career success. We know of many friends and family members who have had similar experiences of their career suffering even though they felt that they were putting in the same number of hours after having a kid. Their career success seemed to be especially impacted if they had their first child closer to their entry into the workforce. Interestingly, men's career success was more independent of parenthood.

Finances

Planning for the future is natural in parenthood. This involves finances, home expansion, insurance, educational choices and expectation over school grades, amongst others. All of these are often associated with anxiety, especially when funds are limited.

The cost of parenting varies from country to country. In the US, it costs around US$233,000 to raise a child till the age of 17. In Australia this would cost about US$180,000. In Singapore the figure ranges between US$190,000 and US$380,000.

The sheer amount of money needed to raise a child naturally brings worry and anxiety for most parents. While this is not a deterrent for most families, it can plunge some families into despair, especially if they want to give their very best to their children.

We have not yet factored in the cost of sending children overseas to pursue their studies or helping out with weddings expenses. We remember a cabbie in his sixties who shared that he had to sell his home so that he could send his daughter to the US to study medicine.

You would probably also need to cater to the financial needs of your own parents, who are probably much older and perhaps even in need of money for their medical needs. Not forgetting yourself in the picture, where you need to plan the finances for your future and old age. It is a cycle, and there is no end to this financial planning, which can destabilise families, particularly when they have limited income.

Future Involvement

As a child grows into a teenager and then an adult, parents shift their anxieties to the child's love partnerships. The level of involvement in the child's marriage depends on the culture. Obviously arranged marriages involve high-level decisions from the parents compared to autonomous marriages.

While it may be a bit early to think about this in your case, it is worth asking yourself a few questions to reflect on the level of involvement you desire to have in your child's future life:

- Would the gender of your child's life partner be a concern for you?

- How about his or her ethnicity or religion?
- What about profession, educational level, nationality, age, or even height?

Your answers to these questions reflect your values, which may in turn be influencing your children, whether explicitly or indirectly. Your child may come to accept these beliefs and values, or may rebel against them. How prepared are you for the latter outcome?

I (Sunita) remember having a conversation with my friends about their reactions if they found out one day that their child preferred same-gender relationships. My friends were strongly against the idea and insisted that it would not happen. They seemed to find it hard to accept. The same reaction could apply to other issues, such as religion or finances. So:

- What do you value as a person?
- What does the family value?
- What do you want your child to value?

* * *

All these challenges are real and normal. While we cannot prevent them from happening, we can certainly do something to manage them through mindfulness, either directly or through the insights we gain from mindfulness practices.

Once-A-Child Syndrome

You were once a child. Your experiences as a child significantly shape the way you create experiences for your own child. If you had a positive childhood experience, then you are likely to re-create those for your child. If you had negative experiences, then you are likely to try your level best to avoid the same with your child.

For example, we have heard our parents tell us that they had a very hard life being brought up in a large family with little to eat or spend. As a result, they ensured that we had enough to eat and grow healthily. They also decided to have smaller families. I (Sunita) remember how my father would repeat over and over again that the only way to influence others and to be out of poverty was to be well-educated. This definitely had an impact on me.

At the same time, there are unconscious habits and behaviours that we may have as a result of our childhood experiences that may influence our current attitudes and actions towards our children. In mindfulness, we want to enhance our self-awareness so that children can grow in a wholesome way.

Let us discuss a couple of these unconscious habits or patterns that are decidedly unhelpful in creating a mindful family.

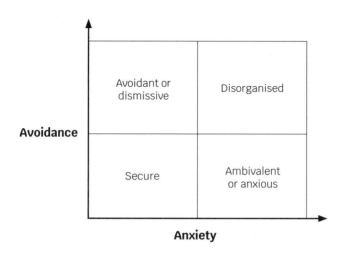

Attachment Theory

The attachment theory developed by John Bowlby is a great source for us to understand ourselves better as a child and an adult.

The attachment theory presents how relationships with parents can impact the healthy development of a child. The theory proposes that there are four styles of attachment in relationships. When a child attaches well to a parent in their infant and childhood years, they also connect well with others when they become an adult. Out of the four attachment styles, only one of them is considered a healthy attachment while the other three are considered unhealthy or insecure attachments.

1. The first of the four is **secure attachment**, which is considered a healthy attachment to a parent. In this style, as a child, you may have developed the ability to feel safe and have

faith in your abilities, as your parents would have nurtured and reassured you. You would be independent and resilient as well. As an adult, you will be able to have close connection and emotional intimacy with your friends, family and loved ones. You will be comfortable working through conflicts, self-regulation and managing expectations of yourself and that of your partner.

What were your parents like? Your parents were probably nurturing, sensitive, supportive and consistent in their way of relating with you as a child. They were probably warm and caring towards you and thus you formed a secure attachment with them.

2. The second style is **avoidant or dismissive attachment**, where you are probably emotionally distant and not very explorative. You will be high on avoidance and low on anxiety. You may feel that your needs will never be met,

feel uncomfortable with emotional closeness, and find it hard to trust others or depend on them. You will be more independent and value freedom. Chances are that your parents were less available in your younger years and were detached and disengaged in parenting.

3. The third style is **ambivalent or anxious attachment**, which is characterised by being high on anxiety but low on avoidance. This style might result in you being angry, inconsistent, unpredictable and neglectful. You want closeness and intimacy but consistently worry that your partner and loved ones will abandon you. You do not feel valued and probably have lower self-esteem. When you were a child, your experience with your parents might have been inconsistent and there could have been a lack of attunement with you.

4. The last style is **disorganised attachment,** where you are mostly depressed, angry, passive or non-responsive. This could also be related to fear. You are probably high on anxiety and also high on avoidance. You constantly worry about your partner's commitment level, feel uncomfortable with intimacy, and find it hard to trust anyone or depend on them. Your parents could have been neglectful and perhaps used fear and anger to manage the relationship. They probably did not have a clear strategy in parenting and they could also have been extreme and abusive as parents.

Be aware of your style. One way is to do an online assessment – there are many free tools available. This may allow you to consciously respond to your child as you continue practising mindfulness and to be aware as to how you can help yourself from unconsciously influencing your child.

Appeasing Your Child

Overly appeasing behaviour, where we seek to satisfy a child's every whim, could also be part of the syndrome. Appeasing can mean that we go all out to make a child feel happy in an attempt to stop their bad behaviour. But by doing so, the child feels that she is being rewarded for the bad behaviour.

For example, we know of friends who pass their smartphones and electronic tablets to their children when the child screams to get their attention or refuses to eat without watching a YouTube video. This is indirectly reinforcing a negative behaviour, which is a form of 'operant conditioning'.

In the theory of operant conditioning, behaviours are either strengthened through rewards or weakened through punishments.

There are two types of rewards: positive and negative. If your child cleans his room every day for a week and you decide to take him out for a movie as a reward, this is a form of positive reinforcement. In the earlier example where the parent gave a screaming child a smartphone to stop the screaming, the parent negatively reinforced the behaviour by removing the unpleasant experience of screaming for the child.

Similarly, there are two types of punishment. In positive punishment, the screaming child might receive a spanking in the hope that he will not scream again in future. In negative punishment, the parent might disallow the child from having their favourite ice cream or movie time.

If you find yourself appeasing your child frequently, perhaps some important questions to ask are:

- Why am I appeasing my child?
- What needs of mine am I fulfilling?
- How can my child learn from this experience without the need to be appeased?

Aggression

Aggression can best be defined as feelings of anger and hostility. Some of us may be naturally aggressive in our words and actions. It can also manifest as violent behaviour and being confrontational.

Aggression in parents usually results in disciplining harshly, humiliating your child, overly controlling the child by using fear, or screaming and raising your voice and even physically hurting your child.

Doing any of these may influence a child negatively. The child may form insecure attachment and may become an aggressive adult herself or even a bully. Or, she could also become timid, fearful, anxious and easily intimidated.

Managing the tendency to be aggressive is challenging because we may not have the skills to do so. Our awareness levels are at the lowest when we are angry. The emotional part of the brain, the amygdala, has hijacked the brain, while the prefrontal cortex – the decision-making part – is unable to function well.

Fortunately, this behaviour can be managed through enhanced awareness, compassion and kindness.

Punishment

There is another trait we possess, which is the need to punish a child when he or she misbehaves. The whole premise of punishment is to use an action which is usually painful as a means to deter someone from doing the wrong thing. Punishment is also something we use to induce regret and remorse.

In 2011, an interesting research was carried out with American children aged 6–10 to find out which method worked best as a means of disciplining children: spanking, reasoning, withdrawing privileges, or time-outs. Reasoning was rated the fairest method, and spanking the least fair. But spanking was found to be the most effective for immediate compliance, though it was not effective for long-term change. Reasoning was found to be the preferred method for long-term change.

Although more studies are needed to confirm this, it is quite clear that both punishment and reasoning can be used very mindfully.

We are not encouraging you to spank your children, but what we are stating is that your punishment may not always work or it may create the opposite effect in the way the child perceives and receives it. From a mindfulness perspective, what we need is the awareness that we are punishing for a reason.

- Is it because you were punished as a child and it worked so it should work now?
- Is it because it takes less time and effort so we might as well punish?
- Is it because we do not know what else would change the child's behaviour?

Your answers to these questions will reveal more about why you are doing what you are doing. Perhaps what is more important is that you bring compassion and kindness to your response instead of punishment. Punishment is often an autopilot reaction. And after punishing the child, some parents feel regret, and end up 'making up' to the child with toys or in other ways.

On the other hand, if you punish your child with total awareness that you are punishing with a reason, in the interest of the child's well-being, you will only feel compassion and calmness, without an ounce of regret.

Labelling

Many of us have this tendency to label our children. This could be because we were labelled as children ourselves. The problem with labelling is that it can stay with the child forever. We have met many adults who loosely label themselves or others as ADHD, stupid, impulsive, etc. These labels have stayed with them all their lives.

The positive aspects of diagnostic labelling such as ADHD, ODD, dyslexic and others, allow us to help children to learn and grow healthily. But these labels can also become negative when they become a stigma. We need to be aware that when we use such labels, they can become fateful and will not help our children rise above it. Therefore, they should only be used for the purpose of providing psychological and counselling interventions and for learning needs.

Outside of these situations, repeating the label again and again only reinforces what is not wholesome and eventually the child believes that they are just that label and nothing more. Telling a child constantly that he has ADHD only makes the child think that he is different and unacceptable or perhaps a mistake or misfit in life. How is that ever helpful?

What if, instead of a label, we used descriptive words to talk about challenges and ways around it? The conversation would now be very different. There is no labelling and instead there is a way forward.

At the same time, we are not asking you to use only positive descriptions. This can have the effect of making a child narcissistic. What we want a child to recognise is that she has the capacity to be a good human being. This is possibly the best label anyone could accept with all of their vulnerabilities and strengths.

Achievements

How do you feel about your children's achievements? Some of you may have experienced your parents being filled with pride when you excelled in your exams or won a prize in a competition. Do you look forward to your children making similar achievements?

While this can certainly be a positive aspiration, sometimes such needs can become an obstacle to your child's development. The pride that we hope to experience could stem from our own unmet needs and desires. We try to compensate by making our children achieve these goals instead.

For example, if I didn't have the chance to go to university, I might set that as a goal for my child and pressure him to achieve it, so that I can be part of that success. My (Sunita) parents are illiterate but they constantly encouraged my siblings and me to study hard. That might have been their way of achieving their unmet needs of having an education. It was an especially sore point for my father. He did not have an education as he had to come to Singapore at a young age to work. He achieved a lot nevertheless, but this desire lingered at the back of his mind. This is how we create a proxy through which we feel good about ourselves and our family.

Many a time, when parents talk about their children, they talk about their academic or professional achievements. These achievements make the parents feel good about themselves – regardless of whether their children felt good about it.

It is wiser to see if your children would benefit more by using their innate strengths, abilities and interests.

One of my (Sunita) clients told me how she encouraged her children to choose careers that they were interested in rather than what she wanted for them. Personally she preferred for them to be bankers or entrepreneurs but she recognised that it would be unfair to impose these preferences on them. Her children are now exploring careers as an artist, nurse and counsellor. Initially, she was worried about how they would cope financially (as she considered these low-paying jobs), but ultimately she felt that as a mother, she should support their dreams and give them the freedom to explore, or else their life lessons would not be valuable.

Children's Challenges

Let us now change perspective and discuss some of the challenges that children may experience. Although standards of living have gone up tremendously in the past decades, the internal world of children may not be as developed. Children across the globe today are facing a unique set of challenges.

Inferiority and Superiority Complex

Firstly, we find that children today are more aware of social class. Researchers in Scotland found that children between the ages of 5 and 7 were unconsciously judging themselves about their social class differences even at that early stage in life.

Children notice that not all of their friends attend enrichment activities or have meals at expensive restaurants. What research informs us is that the choices that parents make on a daily basis such as the types of schools, enrichment programmes or social gatherings that their children engage in more or less determine their children's social class. Children become affected by the way parents behave and the choices they make on behalf of the children.

Social class differences also influence parents, for example in deciding who their children should play with during their breaks in schools. The schools their children attend further deepen these perceptions. For instance, children that go to private schools may not want to be friends or be associated with children who go to public schools.

I (Sunita) remember conducting a life skills programme in a primary school once, and one of the students asked me if I drove to the school. When I said that I did not drive and took a bus to the school, he gave me a confused look and said that each of his parents had a car and so did his teacher. He asked me to get a car, as they were cheap, so I wouldn't need to walk in the hot sun. While I was grateful for his thoughtfulness, I was concerned by his thinking and what values he might be holding. Imagine the plight of children who develop either an inferiority or superiority complex as a result of such conversations.

Social Conformity

As children grow, their identity evolves. They also learn that very often, conformity is required, for example in order to be accepted into a clique at school. They may start emulating the behaviours of their peers, from changing their hairstyles to changing their vocabulary. At this stage in their development, children are looking for an identity.

According Erik Erikson, children start to form identities around the age of 12. Preceding this stage is the stage self-judgement, where the child evaluates his own competence. This tells us that a child's evaluation of his competence can shape his eventual identity.

What we want are children who are comfortable and accepting of themselves and who can find a healthy identity that does not exaggerate what they have or how they look, but instead hold their identity with confidence. This happens from a belief that 'I am OK and good enough as I am. I do not need everyone's approval to look, speak or think in a certain way.'

The challenge that this throws to parenting is that you are now responsible for making your child feel good at her current level of competence so that she does not feel inferior, and yet you need to concurrently encourage her to push her limits. Achieving that fine balance is a skill. When it does not happen, the child becomes confused, which then leads to her conforming to the identity of their peers for social acceptance and comfort. The child's own identity is lost.

Being Controlled

When there is too much control in children's lives, they are at risk of imploding. Especially when their privacy is intruded on, they experience deep confusion. Excessive control also results in the child being more dependent on their parents rather than on themselves.

In 2015, a report on a longitudinal study from the 1940s found that children with over-controlling parents suffered lifelong psychological damage, with many of them reporting low levels of happiness and well-being. The impact was in fact equal to a person suffering from the loss of a loved one.

Often, these controlling behaviours come from the parents' internal need to solve their own issues. The thing about control is that we are unable to let go of the need to control. It happens so unconsciously that you do not even know it. But the damage is done to the child, as well as to people around you.

How can we learn to let things be as they are? How do we learn acceptance?

Emotional Transference

Emotional transference is another issue that children face. This refers to the transfer of emotions experienced by parents to their children. Children notice their parents' emotions – consciously and unconsciously – and re-create them within themselves. A simple example would be that when your child senses that you are sad, she feels sad too.

Research has shown that parents with depression, when trying to adapt to it using unwholesome means, can cause their children to develop their own emotional problems.

However, it is easier said than done when it comes to regulating our emotions. For example, it is natural for you to be worried and

anxious if your child falls ill for a prolonged period of time. Your emotions would be felt by your child. While your emotions are not going to help him, it is natural for you to feel the way you are feeling. Trying to portray a positive emotion in times like these is not easy.

We need to also recognise that the child is noticing not just the emotions but also what the emotions prompt you to do, including your facial expressions, tone of voice and posture. Your child learns to connect these responses to a particular emotion and in future, they might repeat it unconsciously.

These interpretations take place with both positive and negative emotions. And between the two, it is the negative emotions that we are more concerned about, since we know that people remember and replay negative situations and emotions a lot more than they do the positives.

For example, I (Sunita) remember once being scolded by a teacher in primary school for not handing in my homework. I was very upset with her as I felt that she had publicly shamed me. I held on to the shame and anger for days. In that instance, I had forgotten all the times when the teacher had helped me or was kind to me. I replayed only the negative incidents and escalated my negative feelings towards her.

The more frequently you demonstrate negative emotions, the greater is the impact on your children. The frequency of these occurrences gets interpreted by them as the norm, which eventually becomes an unconscious behaviour on their part. These interpretations can start in children as young as three years old.

Children See, Children Do

Your child notices everything you do and will do the same in due course. If you lie, they will probably lie too. If you treat your spouse badly, they will probably do the same to their spouse. Of course, this applies to the good too. If you are kind, they will probably also be kind. If you speak the truth, they will too.

Just as in the case of emotional transference, bear in mind that the frequency of occurrence and the immediacy of its impact are what children hold on to.

* * *

We have now briefly touched on the various challenges that parents and children face. At this point you may feel that they are hard to surmount. What matters, though, is that you have the best interests of your children at heart. Give yourself credit for doing all that has brought you to this present moment.

In the following chapters, we will look at how to create the mindful family that you desire without judging yourself.

Sitting Meditation

The purpose of this practice is to simply be with yourself and look within. This is an opportunity for you to be in a state of being as opposed to being in a state of doing. You could also use an audio practice file (available on the internet) to guide you. Pick one that is 10–15 minutes long if this is your first time attempting this meditation.

1. Adopt a comfortable sitting position which keeps your back upright and relaxed.

2. Close your eyes and bring your attention to your breathing.

3. Do not manipulate or change your breath in any way. Simply be aware of it.

4. Observe your breath deep down in your belly. Feel your abdomen as it expands gently on the in-breath and falls back on the out-breath.

5. Every time you find your mind wandering, just gently bring it back to the breath.

6. Now, as you observe your breathing, you may find from time to time that you are becoming aware of sensations in your body. Notice the body with curiosity.

7. As you maintain awareness of your breathing, expand the awareness to observe your body, from head to toe, and notice all the sensations. Be here with whatever feelings and sensations that may arise from time to time without judging them.

8. With your breathing and body in the background of your awareness, expand your awareness to include your thoughts as they move through your mind. Observe them as they rise, linger and dissolve on their own. Notice the thoughts from moment to moment, even as new thoughts come and go. Thoughts are just thoughts. You need not avoid, reject or pursue them. Just notice them with curiosity.

9. As the meditation ends, give yourself credit for having spent this time in a state of being.

Sitting Meditation

(Mindfulness of positive moments)

This practice is to be guided by a parent. We have a recommended script below, but feel free to adapt it as you feel necessary. You'll need an exercise/yoga mat, or you can also use a bed for your child to lie down on.

1. Lie down on your back. Let your legs and your arms relax and fall to the sides. Make yourself comfortable and close your eyes.

2. Begin to notice what is happening in your body with each breath you take. Each time you breathe, notice your belly rising and falling.

3. Gently place your right hand on your chest and your left hand on your belly and feel your chest and belly rise and fall with each in-breath and out-breath.

4. Each time you breathe, your belly rises and falls. See if you can count ten breaths that way. If you lose count, that's OK. Don't judge yourself for that. It happens to everyone. Come back to whatever number you last remember.

5. Now shift your attention to your day today. Think about something that went well or that was fun. What happened? Who was involved?

What did you do? Or perhaps you just enjoyed being there?

6. Now, picture something about yourself that makes you feel good. It could be something you did for someone, or something positive you said to someone, or something you achieved. Picture that in your mind.

7. Now, picture a happy moment. It could be a birthday party or an outing with your family or friends. Picture the people who are there and what is happening.

8. Now, bring someone to mind who makes you happy or makes your laugh. Picture that person – or you could picture your pet too – with your thoughts.

9. Letting go of this person or pet, turn your attention back to your breathing. As your belly rises and falls, see if you can count ten breaths that way.

10. As this practice ends, you may want to wiggle your toes and fingers. Open your eyes and continue to notice the pleasant moments in your life.

CHAPTER 5

What Are My Intentions?

Let us now shift our focus to creating a clear intention for yourself as we unfold the mindfulness way to realising your purpose statement. Like the lens of a camera, let's zoom in on the areas of our lives where we want to make a difference.

Your focusing abilities will be greatly accentuated by the mindfulness practices which we hope you and your child have already started practising. Even if you haven't, it's never too late to start. Mindfulness practices enhance attentional capabilities, so that you notice things more clearly at a cognitive level.

Ten Intentions of Mindful Parenting

Jon Kabat-Zinn and Myla Kabat-Zinn outlined seven intentions of mindful parenting. These intentions can help us focus and be attentive to the goal of creating mindful families. Let us spend some time to reflect on these intentions:

1. To see parenting as an intentional practice, a way of being in a relationship to experience countless opportunities to cultivate self-awareness, wisdom and open-heartedness.

2. To see parenting as an opportunity to embody what is deepest and best in yourself and express it with your children and in the world.

3. To bring greater mindfulness and discernment into your daily life, especially with your children, using awareness of your body and your breathing to ground yourself in the present moment.

4. To remember to see and accept your children as they are, and not simply through the lens of your expectations and fears.

5. To try to see things from each child's point of view and understand what your children's needs are, meeting them as best as you can. This includes keeping in mind their need to learn by doing things on their own, and their need to come up against immovable limits at times.

6. To see that whatever arises in your own life and in the lives of your children, including the dark, difficult, and stressful times, as 'grist for the mill', allowing it to deepen your capacity for empathy and compassion, including for yourself.

7. To bring these intentions into your heart and commit yourself to putting them into practice as best as you can, in way that honours your children's sovereignty and your own.

Over and above these meaningful and pragmatic intentions we have added three more:

8. To facilitate the discovery of wisdom in yourself and in your children.

9. To facilitate the realisation of the value of wholesomeness for yourself and for your children by modelling it.

10. To nurture a climate in the family where everyone thrives through purpose and meaning.

Wisdom

We define wisdom as the assimilated knowledge of seeing the self, others and the world as connected and interdependent. This connection that we recognise is not something religious or exclusively spiritual. The wisdom that we are all connected is humanistic. This wisdom is also the culmination of mindfulness practices and our responses, and it significantly impacts our attitude and well-being. This wisdom cannot be forced or faked. It is dispositional. And yet, we can practise mindfulness and consciously build on this wisdom to shape the outcomes we want.

It is essential that we distinguish humanistic wisdom from the more popular one known as esoteric wisdom. Esoteric wisdom is that which is understood only by a few. More often than not, it is born of religious or philosophical inspiration. The rare few who gain esoteric wisdom usually lead deeply meaningful lives that keep others in awe or inspire the masses.

Humanistic wisdom, on the other hand, is the wisdom born of insights and gained through self-effort. It is always available to all human beings. It is also not bereft of the fundamental moral values such as truth, compassion and love that bind all human beings. This is the wisdom that mindful families can benefit from. Throughout this book, the word 'wisdom' will refer to humanistic wisdom.

You can recognise a wise person when her thoughts, feelings and actions arise from her Being. In spite of having wisdom, a wise person views herself as a simple human being and acts with wholesomeness. She recognises at all times the fundamental human desire to be whole, complete and happy.

The first way that mindfulness supports the realisation of wisdom is by acting as a catalyst for our ability to be aware, pay attention and accept the realities of life. The second role that mindfulness plays is through the mode of curious inquiry and introspection while you are parenting and practising mindfulness. This gives rise to humility and keeps you always curious as you inspire and guide your children. The third role that mindfulness plays is by generating insights. As we practise mindfulness, we start to see things more clearly through the insights generated from our thoughts, emotions and actions.

Wholesomeness

Wisdom recognises the value of being wholesome. Wholesomeness is about acting towards achieving well-being in every aspect of our life and contributing from that intention to the people around us and to the world we live in.

A mindful parent and child see this value clearly from within, without any external motivation or reward. Being wholesome is natural, just like how fruit trees bear fruit for their own benefit and the benefit of others. It is not just about doing things right, but doing the right thing. Both the means and the ends matter.

Well-being is always an inevitable outcome of wholesomeness. Modelling wholesomeness in thoughts, emotions and actions allows your family to achieve and sustain well-being.

Here is a model that I (Sunita) developed for well-being that you can use as a guide to understand how to act wholesomely.

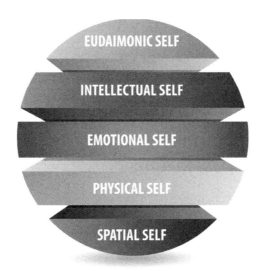

Integrated Well-being Model (IWM)

The Integrated Well-being Model (IWM) provides a systematic approach to achieving well-being for you and your family. Well-being is not just about being happy but about catering to your innate needs at multiple levels. Well-being becomes complete when you satisfy the needs at all five levels of your Self.

The first level is the **Spatial Self**. This is related to the space and environment that our families live in and also to our physical bodies.

Let us start with your environment. Does the space that you live in enhance your well-being? How are the living areas, bedrooms and garden designed to cater to each of your individual and family needs? Where does the family gather to spend time together and how is that space designed? We know, for example,

that plants in the home can positively impact the occupants' mood, while water features create a calming effect.

Apart from the home environment, think of the times that the family takes a holiday, for a change of scene. How often does the family go on vacation? We know that even a short vacation can have a positive impact on our well-being for a couple of weeks. Yes, it is not a long-term solution, but it does have a positive impact.

Now, let us shift our focus to the body. How does each family member feel about their body image? How do we care for our body? How is the family supporting each other in their self-care? How do the colours of our home and our clothes impact our well-being? For example, if we wanted to feel cheerful, we could wear yellow on that day and it would also catch people's attention. Of course, your children might prefer wearing black as it makes them feel more confident and that too is fine.

The idea here is to negotiate as a family to balance the common spaces and the individual spaces while allowing some level of individuality. The space and environment that we live in do have an impact on our well-being and so does our relationship with our body.

The second level is the **Physical Self**, which we can analyse via two components: physical activity and physiological health. Does your family spend time in energising and physically nourishing activities? How frequently does this happen? What about managing the level of energy throughout the day? How does the family exercise? Research shows that individuals who exercise have better well-being.

Moving on to the physiological aspect, how is the family's health? Do you eat nourishing food and drinks? What diet choices does each person have? If someone in the family has a diet that is different from the rest, such as veganism, can the family support and cater to those needs? How does the family relax? How about sleep patterns and quality of sleep?

Our physical body has a positive impact on our overall well-being. And some of our unwholesome habits such as not caring for our body or not sleeping enough (optimally 7.5–9 hours) can sometimes stand in the way of achieving well-being at this level.

The third level is the **Emotional Self**. What emotions are frequently experienced in your family? Happiness, enthusiasm and contentment? Or sadness, dissatisfaction and anger? What activities in the family bring positive emotional experiences? What support does each family member need for emotional regulation? How capable is the family of recognising each other's emotions and responding appropriately? What about being in touch with their own emotions? What are some acceptable ways to express emotion within the family? These questions tell us about the emotional climate of the family and whether they are transient or perpetual.

The fourth level is the **Intellectual Self**. This is related to the ability of families to achieve their life and family goals with competence. It refers to a cluster of competencies such as skills, knowledge, values, strengths, control, decision-making, spirituality, personality and relationships, amongst others.

This is a key component of well-being in families, especially when parents lag behind the capabilities of their children. Parents need to know how to use new gadgets and devices as much as their children. And it extends to even having the ability to coach and guide everyone in the family with skills. When it comes to relationships, more than just intention, we also need the skills of using our words and behaviour to nurture our relationships.

The fifth and final level is the **Eudaimonic Self**, which focuses on purpose and meaning. While the purpose of life for many people is happiness, meaning is what we create for ourselves to achieve that purpose. We have a choice to create meaning in our lives by choosing to engage in the activities that bring the most happiness and wholesomeness to ourselves and others.

As a family, your life can become meaningful too. But do you know what creates meaning for everyone in your family and also as a family? You can help your younger children find their meaning by noticing their inclinations and nurturing them with non-judgemental inquiry.

For example, your child may enjoy playing with the cats in your neighbourhood and may feel very upset if someone abuses the cats. As a parent, you can have a conversation around your child's feelings and see if he feels very strongly about the welfare of cats. If so, you might then consider helping your child to volunteer with a cat welfare organisation and see if that is meaningful to him. Does he feel happy and connected taking part in these activities? Does he talk about his involvement with excitement?

Another dimension of meaning is how we help each other create more meaning in our lives. It is good to have conversations with your family members about what makes their life meaningful and help them achieve it in ways that are possible for the family. In fact, parenting too can be one of prime meaning if we know exactly how that would help us in being happy. We know that people who live their lives with a clear sense of purpose and meaning have better well-being, and the same applies to the entire family.

A good way to understand that which is unwholesome is by looking at the opposite of what the five Selves represent. Imagine a family life where your

- Home is unkempt, disorganised, unhygienic, cluttered.
- Clothes are dirty, unwashed, smelly.
- Lifestyle is sedentary, with hours spent in front of the TV.
- Emotional climate is constantly sad, worrying, frightening or anxious.
- Skills are limited and you are unable to cope with life's demands.
- Relationships lack effective communication and lack connection. Everyone does their own thing.

- Life has no meaning. No one knows why they're doing what they're doing. Every day is devoid of excitement.

Perhaps now you can see how the IWM is a very powerful, comprehensive and systematic approach to working towards achieving well-being for you and your family. With this model in mind, we can intentionally lead our families towards enhanced well-being.

Hedonic Satisfaction

Returning to the topic of wholesomeness, we are now going to talk about a big misconception. There is this pervasive belief that our lives need to be satisfying and sensorially engaging. This belief can sometimes create the need for 'hedonic' satisfaction. We have met people with this incessant need for sensory satisfaction. As a result, they and their family are always expecting positive emotions and experiences, and unable to accept negative or painful experiences.

The truth, however, is that meaningful and intellectual activities and experiences may not always create positive emotions. One of the most meaningful experiences of a human being is childbirth. But childbirth can be very painful and emotionally draining. Therefore, wholesomeness is not just about sensory and emotional satisfaction.

The Subjectivity of Good

People tend to use the word 'good' quite loosely with things that are supposedly wholesome. Most often the word 'good' leaves room for much subjectivity. Something might be good for one person but bad for another. It depends on many factors such as our likes, dislikes, moral beliefs, and favourable outcomes, amongst others. For example, fast food is considered good because it tastes good for many people and yet it is also considered bad as it is unhealthy, especially if consumed frequently.

Therefore, instead of relying on the subjectivity of good, it is important that we are able to identify *why* something is good. This requires conversations in the family as well as patience and willingness to explore such subjectivity.

Boundaries

Wholesomeness also includes appropriate boundaries for everyone in the family. There are several types of boundaries: developmental, family, social and cultural.

Developmental boundaries are those that limit your child's behaviour. A simple example would be physical intimacy that may not be acceptable in the early years but acceptable when they become adults.

Family boundaries are passed on from generation to generation and include addressing elders in a particular way and perhaps even not calling certain categories of people by their personal names.

Social boundaries are norms and even laws that are accepted by a group of people. It allows children to understand that they live with other people in society and that certain norms help people to co-exist respectfully and harmoniously.

Cultural boundaries are those that are based on the values and beliefs of a community, for example in religious settings. The behaviour expected in such settings is important for children as they grow.

Boundaries help children to become adults with a sense of security and awareness of their own boundaries and an appreciation of other people's boundaries.

Social Skills

The significant impact of children's social skills cannot be understated. With healthy self-esteem, they are more socially responsible and also accept themselves when relating to others, holding their space with confidence while allowing others to hold theirs. We can also expect more pro-social behaviours when children act from a space of spontaneous compassion, kindness and empathy. Nurture your child to manifest these more consciously through reinforcement and daily mindfulness practices as a family.

Measuring Life Through Intrinsic Value

One of the important intentions to set for ourselves is the way we measure our life's success. In 2010, Clayton Christensen, a professor at Harvard Business School, addressed the graduating class. He had recently been diagnosed with cancer, and in his address he posed the graduating students three questions:

1. How can I be sure that I'll be happy in my career?

2. How can I be sure that my relationships with my spouse and my family become an enduring source of happiness?

3. How can I be sure I'll stay out of jail?

Christensen passed away in 2020, but his questions continue to resonate. We often tend to measure success by economic value. For many of us, our life revolves around how much money we are making or how rich we are. Is this really a measure of success? What defines success in your family? In truth, our intrinsic value lies in who we are and what we give, not in what we have.

We would like to add two more questions to the list above:

4. How can I be of service to the world?

5. How can I bring well-being to my five Selves and my family members' five Selves?

Let's encourage our children to pay attention to the fact that as simple human beings, what's really important to us is well-being, happiness, relationships, being a good citizen and being of service to others. Constantly reinforce even the smallest contribution from your child towards these five goals, and avoid assigning any economic value to them. These five goals are lifelong goals.

Living is a Meditation

When executed well, these intentions allow parents to help their children build self-esteem by having a self-concept that extends beyond just their self. The relational dimension of wisdom helps children to see themselves with positive regard without narcissism. With healthy self-esteem, children find it easier to relate with others and with the world they are in. This is carried right through to their adulthood.

When we align our thoughts, words and actions with clear intention, enabled by mindfulness practices, our life can become a meditation in itself. We can then constantly bring awareness, acceptance and attention to our life with a dispositional behaviour.

Parenting, too, becomes like a meditation – not a closed-eyes affair but a disposition that allows you to parent from a space of self-awareness. And when your children see you modelling it, they learn by example. They witness you practising mindfulness consistently, and they connect your behaviour with the practice. This can be very empowering and inspiring to your child. Imagine being the superhero for your child. Such is the effectiveness of mindfulness in your family.

Having now looked at these intentions, we would like you to take this opportunity to review your parenting purpose statement, in case you would like to incorporate some of the new intentions discussed in this chapter.

Your updated purpose statement:

Mindful Walking

Being mindful in walking integrates mind-fulness into your daily life. Mindful Walking is not about arriving at your destination or rushing to finish your walk, but simply being mindful that you are walking and that you are breathing. Walk in a leisurely and peaceful manner, with gentle breathing and curiosity. We arrive with every step. Mindful Walking can be practised together with your child.

1. Try this practice without your shoes or socks on.

2. Begin your walk by mentally stating that 'I am starting this walk'.

3. Walk with eyes your on the ground about 7–8 steps ahead of you.

4. Feel the sensation of each foot as it presses down onto the earth or floor.

5. Notice your foot as it lifts up, touches the ground and is lifted up again. Follow the movement and the feeling of each footstep with your mind and your breath.

6. Notice which part of your foot leaves the ground and which part strikes the ground first at the beginning of each step.

7. Try walking faster for a few seconds and notice how your feet feel.

8. Now slow down and notice the difference in your heartbeat, breath and bodily sensations.

9. Walk slowly until you come to a pause. As you stand in stillness, notice the sensations in your feet and the weight of your body on your feet.

10. As you end this practice, bring the aware-ness of your walk into the rest of the day.

CHAPTER 6

How is Mindfulness Psychological Capital for My Family?

In this chapter, let's talk about the 'psychological capital' that mindfulness can create in your family. Like financial capital, psychological capital appreciates over time when invested mindfully. The investment in the case of mindfulness is basically consistent practice and learning from the insights that you gain. And the yield is well-being for you and your family.

There isn't a family that exists without any challenges. However, how we cope with these challenges individually and as a family determines our growth. Parents who play a pivotal role in shaping mindful families create wisdom and self-understanding, and enjoy psychological freedom within the family and society.

In Chapter 2, we learned about the Triangle of Mindfulness and the 3 A's of Awareness, Acceptance and Attention. Let us discuss how these 3A's – or the lack of them – pose challenges to building psychological capital in the family.

Awareness

The lack of self-awareness creates a vacuum of self-ignorance in family members. Family members with lowered self-awareness suffer from not being able to monitor their stress levels, thoughts, emotions, bodily responses and beliefs. We cannot understate how these mental conditions influence our actions and behaviours.

All of us know that stress creates psychological strain such as confusion, anxiety and even depression. Physical effects include cardiovascular disease, high blood pressure, heart attacks and even stroke. Imagine the effects of these on your health and that of your family.

Not being aware of our thoughts is another aspect of low self-awareness. It's like being on autopilot, where we don't notice that what we're thinking, saying or doing is being influenced by automatic thoughts. This phenomenon becomes more pronounced when we are triggered by a situation or an event. Our habitual reactions then kick into action and we create a vicious cycle of automatic thoughts that guide action and end up perpetuating it.

Bodily Sensations and Emotions

Noticing our body's sensations and responses is another aspect of self-awareness. Our emotions manifest themselves in our bodies. In a research study by Finnish scientists in 2014, it was found that people across cultures had very similar bodily reactions to emotions, as measured by changes in heart rate, breathing patterns and limb activity.

For example, anxiety is often be experienced as pain in the chest, while happiness triggers warm, pleasurable sensations all over the body. Depression manifests itself as a deadening of feeling in the arms and legs.

Yet sometimes, even though our body is responding, mentally we don't register the emotion or recognise its intensity. If these emotions frequently centre around fear, anger, disgust, anxiety or shame, this can have an adverse effect on our physical health, from weakening our immune system to damaging our heart health. It is like having the car engine on or idling for the whole day and yet not expecting the fuel to run out. There is wear and tear to the body when we experience too many negative emotions daily.

Having noticed our bodily responses, the next step is the ability to interpret the underlying emotions clearly. Otherwise, we may still end up acting in a way that lowers our well-being and that of our family.

Our Beliefs

Awareness of our beliefs has a significant impact on the way we live. By beliefs, we are not confining ourselves to religious beliefs but rather any idea that we accept as truth. If we believed, for example, that everything on earth is meant for our exploitation, then we would ceaselessly consume with no regard for the future.

Our beliefs determine the type and quality of our thoughts, emotions and actions. Our actions then reinforce our beliefs:

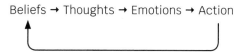

Beliefs → Thoughts → Emotions → Action

Once formed, beliefs are hard to change, even in light of new knowledge. Why does this happen? First, we tend to focus on and give greater credibility to data that supports our current beliefs, ignoring any evidence to the contrary. This is known as confirmation bias. Secondly, we might even consciously invest time and energy trying to disprove any information that contradicts our current beliefs. This is known as disconfirmation bias. These two biases compromise our ability to think logically and objectively.

Try and imagine how it might impact our families if we were to lack this skill of being aware of our beliefs and being able to change our beliefs in light of new evidence.

What if your child believes that you as a parent are only interested in her school grades? This can give rise to the thought that you do not care about her and in turn give rise to the emotions of sadness, anxiety or anger. This can lead your child to do things that may be unfavourable such as giving up on her studies to rebel against you. And when you scold her for not focusing on her studies, it will merely reinforce her earlier thinking that you do not love her and only care about her grades. It becomes a vicious cycle.

How does one break this cycle? The first step is to have awareness of one's beliefs. Everything else that you do to change your beliefs, whatever method that may be, still rests on your self-awareness for its effectiveness.

Meaning

Meaning is one of the most significant things that awareness can bring. The lack of meaning can make our lives feel purposeless. Our interest in daily living depends on our meaning in life. Meaning is something we create for ourselves. Thus, it is not the same for everyone.

Meaning is also something that we discover as we enter adulthood. In early childhood, it is harder to discover meaning. Yet, as a parent, you can pave the path for your child to discover their own meaning in time.

When any family member feels their life has no meaning, or feels that they are useless and unimportant, then family life becomes uninteresting for them. They will look for this usefulness and importance outside of the family.

During our tenure as volunteer prison counsellors, we met teenagers who had been placed behind bars after mixing with unwholesome company. Being part of these groups boosted their self-esteem and made them feel connected to others – feelings that weren't able to find at home. The leaders of these groups were thus able to get the teens to do things that made them feel useful even if they were unwholesome, from peddling drugs to gang fights. The absence of meaning within the family had created a vacuum that compelled these youths to look for it elsewhere.

* * *

With greater self-awareness, we can live life with reduced psychological strain, better health, reduced habitual behaviour, make much better decisions with healthier belief systems and create meaning.

Self-awareness, because it is a psychological skill and a disposition that is lodged deep within our minds, is not easy to cultivate. This is exactly where mindfulness helps. Countless research findings inform us that practising mindfulness helps enhance self-awareness.

If every family member could be more self-aware, can you imagine what a difference it would make in creating a more mindful family and society?

Acceptance

Acceptance is the invitation of all experiences – including discomfort, distractions, rumination – with a sense of accommodation, without any kind of judgement. Every mindfulness practice involves the component of acceptance and also builds towards creating the psychological capacity to be non-reactive and to instead respond with poise even in the most stressful situations.

Maintaining Equanimity

One of biggest challenges for all of us is maintaining equanimity in the face of challenges. The absence of equanimity usually leads to dissatisfaction, rejection, irritation, frustration and disappointments. These feelings are very much there in families, even in the smallest of things such as not lifting the toilet seat, not putting back the remote control, or not helping with the household chores.

Initially, parents may experience these feelings silently, but over time they get expressed through words and actions, especially when no change happens. I (Kathir) remember some of my friends' parents saying to them, 'I regret having you' or 'I hate you'. Of course, these statements were made in the heat of anger and the parents didn't mean it. But such statements can create a permanent dent in children's minds. Years later, your children may say the same things back to you when you become dependent on them, or they may say it to their own children. These are the reactive behaviours when acceptance is not present.

Another dimension of reactivity is related to how we have been 'conditioned' to react to certain stimuli. According to the theory of classical conditioning, we learn through the association of two stimuli that are linked together. For example, if your child saw a lizard in a drawer and felt traumatised by it, she might refuse to open all drawers out of fear of lizards, even if there are no lizards in the next ten drawers. She has linked drawers with the fear of lizards.

One of my (Sunita) clients had difficulty sleeping in the dark for many years. She was fearful that in the darkness, ghosts would attack her. She had picked up this fear from watching a scary movie (stimuli with visuals and sound effects). She shared with me in sessions that no one understood her challenges and kept asking her to grow up. She was in her mid-30s when she decided to go for therapy. What was her motivation to get help? She realised that her phobia was affecting her young son. Mindfulness-based psychotherapy helped her to gain insight into how her mind was functioning, especially with anxiety-type stimulus, and how to sit with her fear and anxiety rather than fighting or escaping it. After a couple of months, she was able to sleep with the lights off, and she was most pleased that she did not pass her fear on to her son.

Maintaining equanimity in all situations, including unfavourable ones, is truly important in family relationships and well-being.

Situational Outcomes

Our minds usually find it difficult to accept situations that are not favourable to us. Consider the typical situation when a child brings home his examination results. You might have been expecting him to score nothing less than 90 marks out of 100. However, he returns home with 65 marks. What would your mental state be? Irritation, frustration, unhappiness, disappointment, anger – or acceptance?

I (Sunita) remember one of my teen clients sharing with me: 'Why can't my parents see that I have passed and am an average kid? Why must I be the best? What if I don't want that? What's their problem? I hate them!' I believe you can sense his disappointment and anger with his family. He probably feels unaccepted in his family because of his grades. This may or may not be true but that is how he feels because of his parents' reaction to his grades. It is his perception of reality.

In mindfulness, we say that there is no standard response to a situation like this one. It depends on many factors, such as the sincere effort of the child, the time invested in coaching the child, the emotional investment and the value that you may have over the results, which is highly subjective, amongst many other factors. However, we often fail to take these factors into consideration when confronted with an unfavourable outcome.

Now, you may feel that the root problem is having expectations. However, there is nothing wrong in having expectations. It's perfectly natural. What we need to accept, though, is that outcomes will not always meet our expectations. For every expectation and action, there will be one of the four following outcomes: (1) As expected; (2) Better than expected; (3) Less than expected; and (4) Opposite to what was expected.

For example, you expected your child to score 90 for his test. He might score as you expected (90 marks), he might exceed your expectations (100 marks), he might score less than expected (65 marks), or he might get the opposite of your expectations (12 marks). What would your response to each outcome be? Our usual reaction to 'as expected' outcomes is satisfaction. With 'better than expected' outcomes, we are usually elated. With 'less than expected' outcomes, we are usually

disappointed. And with 'opposite to expected' outcomes, we feel bitter and angry.

Each of these feelings is justified, but what we must be mindful of is how these feelings translate into actions. With acceptance, what happens is that our mind creates a psychological pause between an event and our action. That pause is the equanimity, poise and calmness from which we can then think objectively to act wholesomely.

Event → *Pause* → Action

As Viktor Frankl said: 'Between stimulus and response there is a space. In that space is our power to choose our response. In our response lies our growth and our freedom.'

Self-Acceptance

Self-acceptance is another phenomenon that helps us to create the future we want without striving.

Many a time, we reject aspects of our personality, our physical appearance, or our circumstances. A child may compare herself with her friends, for example in the number of toys she has. Or she may feel that she is fat, and others in the family make her feel that being fat makes her ugly or less worthy.

What is needed in such situations is not comparison but acceptance that each one of us is different. Comparing your family to another family or comparing your children against one another is also an unhealthy exercise.

Take wealth, for example. Some families are wealthy and unhappy. Some are wealthy and happy. Some are poorer in financial wealth but happy together as a family. Families come from different economic backgrounds and there are many factors that contribute to it. Comparing your family with another family economically is quite different from wanting to give your family the basic comforts.

Coming back to the example of the child that may be fatter, instead of making her feel lousy about her weight, it would be a better idea to introduce her to a wholesome lifestyle. We need to support children to feel comfortable in their skin before looking to change them. We can also help them expand their lens rather than zooming in on one area. We want them to be able to accept both the good and the bad.

Researchers and psychologists have for years been showing evidence that parental evaluations can positively or negatively impact a child's level of self-acceptance and self-esteem. Children are only able to accept themselves to the extent that parents make them feel accepted in their life. When parents are unable to express to their children that they are acceptable as they are, children grow up feeling that there is something seriously wrong with them.

By developing self-acceptance, we also develop the ability to accept others. There are four permutations when it comes to self-acceptance and other-acceptance:

- I am not alright. You are not alright.
- I am not alright. You are alright.
- I am alright. You are not alright.
- I am alright. You are alright.

While there are people who are accepting of others but not of themselves, seldom do we meet people who find it difficult to accept others while being able to accept themselves. This tells us that the key to accepting others is first accepting oneself.

Psychologist Robert Holden, who specialises in studying happiness and well-being, states that self-acceptance and happiness go hand in hand. Your family's well-being is dependent on self-acceptance. Your intention is the first step towards self-acceptance, which is why we start mindfulness practices with setting our intentions for our families.

Emotional Maturity

All the dimensions of acceptance lead to emotional maturity. Emotional maturity is defined as the ability to handle adverse situations without unnecessarily escalating them or blaming others. Through emotional maturity, family members can learn not to blame others for unfavourable situations or praise themselves for all favourable outcomes. Instead, we learn to take responsibility for our actions and respond to situations with wisdom.

A 2017 study in Karnataka state, India, found that MBA students who grew up in positive home environments had higher levels of emotional maturity. Another study, from Vietnam, found that the warmth of parents during childhood led to greater emotional maturity in their children. Mindfulness practices help families build emotional maturity through the awareness and acceptance of oneself and others.

I Am Where I Should Be

The other thing about acceptance is that it invites you to accept that you are already where you should be. This attitude allows you to accept yourself as you are and then look at what you can do about it if necessary, instead of rejecting your current state and trying to be someone else.

Learning to accept ourselves as we are helps us to create our future without illusions. For one, we learn not to compare our present self with our past self. You will age and you will not look younger as you grow older. That does not change your capacity to be aware of yourself. While you could say 'I am old', you could also say 'My body is ageing'. There is a certain objectivity and grace in the latter statement.

This is the power of acceptance, which can shape the quality of life in families.

Attention

The attentional dimension of mindfulness cultivated through mindfulness practices can create five important outcomes.

Concentration and Noticing

The first is the ability to concentrate by paying attention to and focusing on the present moment – essentially what is done in all mindfulness practices.

There is a big misconception that concentration practices are about forcing your mind to be fixated on a single object. This is not true. Concentration practices in mindfulness revolve around mentally noticing with awareness and non-judgement. A simple concentration practice would be noticing your breath without changing the way you breathe in the present moment.

During concentration practices, thoughts are not removed, stilled or alleviated. Instead, we acknowledge that it is common for thoughts to be there in our mind and we either notice these thoughts as a neutral observer or we direct our attention to our breath and our physical sensations.

Instead of banishing our thoughts, we develop a sense of curiosity towards them. By doing so, we develop the ability to have a healthy relationship with our thoughts instead of being fearful. We pay attention to both the good thoughts and the bad.

I (Sunita) had a client who kept using music, food and swimming to distract himself whenever he had challenging thoughts as he did not want to see himself as a 'bad' person. But the more he tried to ignore and repress it, the worse it became and he started to dislike this part of him. Through mindfulness-based psychotherapy, however, he learned to stop fighting his thoughts and to face them and accept them.

The more you fight your thoughts, the more you empower them. It is fine to have all types of thoughts, whether positive, negative or neutral, because thoughts do not make an appointment before they arise. They come and go naturally. So the idea of creating a vacuum in the mind without any thoughts is alien to mindfulness.

Strengthening Resolve

The second outcome of attention is strengthening the mind to align with our intentions. For example, we make an intention before going to bed to wake up at 6 a.m. for a jog. And then at 6 a.m. the alarm goes off, and for whatever reason, we do not feel like going for a jog anymore. We hit the snooze button and go back to sleep.

This is very common, where we are unable to find the strength to do what we want to. In 2007, a study of 226 university students found that those who acted mindfully were more likely to put their intentions into action. The attentional component strengthens the mind to work towards achieving your resolutions.

Managing Distractions

The third outcome is the ability to overcome distractions that may happen due to rumination or external stimuli. For example, your child might be studying for her exams when she hears her favourite song in the background. She might become distracted and find it difficult to let go of the involuntary gravitation that the sense of hearing experiences. Or it could be memories of a house party the day before that distract her from focusing on the present moment.

This is a challenge that many people face. However, a 2013 research study on undergraduate students found that after undergoing just two weeks of a mindfulness training programme, there was reduced mind wandering, increased focus, reduced activation of the Default Mode Network, and improved cognitive performance.

Mindfulness practices enhance our ability to focus in the present moment while working on any given task.

Inside-Out Orientation

The fourth outcome is the ability to have an inside-out orientation instead of an outside-in one. This means looking at ourselves first and then looking at the external world in every situation. The absence of this training results in your mind being pulled in all directions by external influences without you having a chance to look at things from your own perspective.

Imagine a child being subjected to peer pressure to do something that may be wrong. Whether or not he succumbs to this pressure

depends on his ability to process it from his own perspective of values and knowledge.

Research on students in Kerala, India, found mindfulness and an internal locus of control to be positively correlated to belief in their abilities and mastery of skills. Similarly, a 2013 study on 310 adults in China found that those who practised mindfulness had more positive core self-evaluations and this led to better life satisfaction.

People who practise mindfulness tend to have greater acceptance of their thoughts, emotions, actions and situations, and do not measure themselves against other people's standards. Developing this skill through mindfulness helps your child and you to constantly process experiences from an inside-out perspective.

Recognition of the Facts of Life

The last aspect of attention we want to talk about is the ability to recognise the instinctive nature of human beings. This constant recognition and recollection, unlike mere awareness, allows us to always acknowledge the facts of life and the values that are common to all human beings – for example, the fact that our purpose is to be happy, or the fact that our thoughts are just thoughts.

This aspect of attention and recollection allows these facts to be on our radar at all times.

* * *

At this point, you would be able to see how the three A's of mindfulness – Awareness, Attention and Acceptance – can impact families. The lack of mindfulness in families leads to unwholesome outcomes and reduces the quality of family life. The simplest way to develop and cultivate these is through the practice of mindfulness, which we will now turn our attention to.

Mindfulness Practices and Attitudes

Mindfulness practices are the foundation on which mindful families are built. The key to creating the life that we want is by increasing the positives in our life while reducing the negatives – and this starts with mindfulness practices.

Everything that we have presented so far in this book and in the pages to come is centred on mindfulness practices. Even the wisdom and insights we spoke about are the fruits of mindfulness practices. Just as you tend to a tree by providing sunlight, water, air and fertiliser, you do the same with mindfulness, by being patient and diligent. The key is to practise mindfulness consistently even if it is for short periods of time. You'll notice that some of the practices are as short as 3 minutes while others are about 30 minutes.

Let us now explore 13 attitudes that are vital to mindfulness practices.

1. Non-Judgement

Paying attention non-judgementally means we do not evaluate the quality of our practice at any point in time. We focus on the practice without judging it as good or bad. Labels have no absolute value. It also means that we do not evaluate or analyse the objects of our practice.

For example, we do not evaluate if our breathing is alright or if it needs to be improved or changed. In psychotherapy, we encourage taking deep breaths when one feels overwhelmed, whereas in mindfulness or mindfulness-based psychotherapy, we encourage directing attention towards the breath but without manipulating it in any way. In fact, by simply noticing your breath, you will realise that it slows down by itself. There is nothing for you to do except pay attention to it as you inhale and exhale naturally.

The same applies to bodily sensations. We do not investigate the sensations that we are noticing in our bodies at this present moment. We accept them as they are and just pay attention to them. We also do not judge our thoughts as they rise and fall in our practice. We just let them be as they are and continue to notice them moment to moment. The same applies to our environment. We notice with curiosity, using all of our senses, rather than making judgements.

2. Inviting All Experiences

We practise acceptance by inviting all experiences into our practice. We do not reject any thought, emotion, sensation or experience. This attitude helps in accommodating and being non-judgemental to experiences.

It is common for our mind to wander or for our body to report discomfort during mindfulness practices. Sometimes our body may even limit our movement. We accept this limitation by doing only what our body allows us to do. There is no perfect movement or posture to come into. Rather, practise within the boundaries of your body with a sense of accommodation. By doing this, you become resilient, and nothing will stop you from practising.

By acceptance, we also mean that you do not compare your practice with your past experiences or with your ideal goal for the future. Also, don't compare yourself against others to see who is getting 'better' at mindfulness. We are all different. The process cannot be sped up. Things will unfold at their own pace. Invite all experiences rather than keeping your eye on specific experiences or results.

3. A Learner's Mind

The learner's mind is one that allows you to learn all the time because you always regard yourself as a beginner, a perpetual work-in-progress. This is the healthy way, rather than thinking you are a success or a failure, which are both judgements.

Even though we have been practising for many years now, each mindfulness practice still gives us new insights about ourselves. We are not experts, and neither are we novices. We are just simple human beings practising mindfulness. This keeps us humble without trying to be humble because there is truly no goal to be reached other than just being who we are and where we are.

4. Focusing on What's Working

Many of us have this habit of trying to fix issues that do not work for us. It is a habit that we have cultivated to solve problems, but the flip side is that we become critical of everything. This habit could stem from a fear of being a failure or being seen as a failure.

In mindfulness, we want to instead cultivate a healthy attitude of focusing on what is working in our life and in our practices rather than what is not. We hold on to that as an anchor as we practise mindfulness. Some of us may feel drawn to certain mindfulness practices and be less interested in other practices. That is fine. Continue to experiment and practise all of them till you are certain that a particular practice works for you and then you can stay with that. There is no right or wrong or good or best. Focus on and do what works for you.

5. Trust

Trust is an important attitude that's required in the practice of mindfulness. We need continuous trust as a practitioner, just like relationships need trust to thrive. Sometimes we may doubt the effectiveness of mindfulness practice because it is something that takes time. And in spite of the plentiful empirical evidence that mindfulness works, our minds may still doubt it. Are we making unreasonable expectations of a practice? This can lower the trust that we have in the process.

In our lives, we have benefited from keeping in mind the success stories of others and people who have sustained the practice. Their journeys can keep us inspired. Experiment with the mindfulness practices and use your own experiences, besides research evidence, as a basis to trust the process and continue practising.

6. Curiosity

When we bring curiosity into our practice of mindfulness, it becomes a means of knowing more about ourselves. What was once in our blind spot will now appear to be so vivid to you. These are insights that you gain about yourself related to your body, thoughts, behaviours and emotions.

As this curiosity gets developed and enhanced, you start to notice changes and intricate details in the environment. You may also start enjoying and appreciating the diversity and similarity of things and people around you. We have found that after each practice, we discover so much more about ourselves.

7. Letting Go

The ability to let go is another important attitude of mindfulness. The opposite of letting go is being in control. Like the space in a room that does not cling on to the things that are taken away or added to it, we too can practise letting go. When a ripened fruit falls from a tree, we do not see the tree struggling to hold on to the fruits. The water in the sea allows all beings to be within it and also does not resist the removal of these beings.

We feel a need for control because it gives us a sense of security, a sense that we can influence outcomes. Or we feel it because we want every experience to be a 'great' experience.

We can learn to free ourselves of this need when we practise mindfulness by letting go of our expectations. Let go of the attachment to your experiences. Accept any experience. Be simply an observer of the experience by letting go of the expectation that only a positive experience is acceptable.

8. Positivity

You do not have to approach mindfulness only because you have a problem, or only when you feel upset or stressed. That would be akin to starting to exercise only when you have a health problem. Instead, if you see exercising as something positive and as contributing to your well-being, then you will naturally make it part of your life. And it will create great value in your life by preventing health problems or at least reducing any negative impact. We encourage you to approach mindfulness with this same positive attitude.

9. Patience

Patience is another important attitude for mindfulness practitioners. Impatience happens when we make a habit of doing things as fast as can, as if we were in a race. If we were to bring this attitude to mindfulness, then it becomes another race.

Mindfulness is like a seed in the ground that takes consistent effort to nurture into a tree. It is very similar to parenting, where you cannot artificially speed up the growth of a child. It will take place gradually and at its own pace. Similarly, the fruit of mindfulness practices may take weeks, months or even years to appear. The key is to cultivate patience with yourself and the results of your actions.

10. Self-Compassion

Just as we should be compassionate towards others, it is also important to be compassionate towards ourselves. We often judge ourselves if we forget to practise mindfulness or if we fail to do what we planned to do. We expect too much of ourselves as practitioners. as if we now have a halo over our head.

But in truth we are simple beings and we may have very deep roots of unwholesome habits from our past. As we practise mindfulness, these habits may emerge and may stunt our practice or even derail us from our best self. Instead of worrying, focus on the practice, which will loosen the hold that these roots have over you. Being kind to yourself will help you immensely in this direction. Compassion for yourself is the beginning of bringing that attitude to everyone else and other beings.

11. Thankfulness

Being thankful is another important attitude. We are grateful to be alive and to be able to practise mindfulness. We have our mind, our breath and our body. These are the greatest gifts of nature. These gifts coupled with our sincere intention are more than enough to practise mindfulness.

Apart from being grateful for the resources we have, we can also recognise the contributions of others that have enabled us to practise mindfulness. These could be your family members, who supported your practice. Bring thankfulness to the smallest of acts that have enabled you to practise today, instead of just focusing on and being thankful for the benefits we receive.

12. Non-Striving

Non-striving might seem abstract to some. Let us explain. In mindfulness, you are not trying to attain a state that you are not already in. The capacity to be mindful is always available to you, in every moment. All that mindfulness practices do is support you to discover your awareness, acceptance and attention – not create it.

If, on the other hand, you think that you are going to 'become' more aware or more accepting and more attentive, then you are certainly going to strive. By having such ideas, you are reinforcing the idea that you are not where you should be. But in fact you are exactly where you are meant to be and you are discovering mindfulness which is already within you.

Although for the purposes of communication we may say that we are 'developing' our awareness, acceptance and attention, it does not mean that these are alien or external to you. All of these are done in the present moment in the practice and not achieved in a distant time. There is really nothing to strive for if you are already where you are.

13. Generosity

Lastly, an attitude of generosity helps us to recognise that we are human beings capable of helping other people, not just ourselves. As we benefit from the fruits of mindfulness practices, we can also contribute positively towards the well-being of others.

Generosity is not to be mistaken as wanting to promote mindfulness to others. Rather, it is about offering help to those who are in pain or experiencing difficulties and distress. Your generosity could take the form of acts of kindness, financial assistance or emotional support that helps to reduce the pain that others are experiencing. Generosity is a fulfilling experience by itself.

* * *

With these 13 attitudes in mind, and consistent practice, we believe you will discover the wisdom inside yourself, and bring wholesomeness to your family.

Commitment to the Practices

People often ask us: How much practice is required to experience the benefits and impact of mindfulness? Between consistency and intensity, the former is more important, which means that consistent practice of 5 minutes daily is more effective than practising 35 minutes once a week. Think of it as similar to health supplements. Taking a multivitamin tablet daily is much more effective than taking seven at a go once a week or once in a while.

Starting your practice of mindfulness slowly and steadily is very important. Try a 5-minute practice daily to begin with, before gradually increasing it to 10 minutes when you feel ready. There is no specific time duration to strive for. This way, you allow yourself to slowly cultivate a new habit.

A more systematic way to learn mindfulness would be to attend one of the many mindfulness-based programmes offered around the world. These include programmes such as Mindfulness-Based Stress Reduction (MBSR), Mindfulness-Based Cognitive Therapy (MBCT), and Mindfulness-Based Well-being Enhancement (MBWE). These courses are led by certified or qualified mindfulness teachers, who will guide you on your journey, typically over the course of 8 weeks. You will be given reading materials and audio guides for home practice. In the case of public classes, you will also get to meet others who are learning along with you, who can provide mutual support along the journey.

Coping Breathing Space

This practice helps you step out of autopilot mode and brings you into an awareness of the present moment. It is especially valuable when your thoughts are starting go into a spiral of negativity. The practice comprises 3 stages, ABC – Awareness, Breathing and Conscious Expansion

Awareness

1. Adopt a comfortable standing posture that keeps your body relaxed and your back upright. Close your eyes when you are ready.

2. Notice the surface on which you are standing and the weight of your body on your feet.

3. Bring your awareness to your body from your toes to your head.

4. Then ask yourself:

- What is my experience right now in my thoughts? Acknowledge these thoughts as mental events.
- What am I feeling? Acknowledge these feelings as they are, without the need to change them.

- What are some bodily sensations I am feeling? Acknowledge and accept your experience.

Breathing

1. Gently redirect your full attention to your breathing.

2. Observe the rising and falling of your belly with every in-breath and out-breath.

3. Whenever your mind drifts, come back to your breathing. Your breath is your anchor.

Conscious Expansion

1. Expand the field of your awareness around your breathing.

2. Include the sense of your body as a whole, from your head down to your toes, and including your posture.

3. When you are ready, open your eyes and continue the day with a sense of stability. Come back to your body and your breath if you ever feel overwhelmed.

Self-Compassion Practice

This practice is to be guided by a parent. We have a recommended script below but feel free to adapt it as you feel necessary.

1. Let us begin by sitting comfortably with your back upright and head facing straight ahead.

2. Gently close your eyes so that you are not distracted by the moving objects around us.

3. Start by taking three deep breaths.

4. As you breathe, bring your attention to how that feels. Notice your belly rising and falling. If it helps, place your right hand on your chest and your left hand on your belly and notice your body's movements.

5. Notice the air moving in and out of your body and having a rhythm of its own as you breathe. Now place your hands on your thighs and let them rest there.

6. Now, think of a situation in your life that is difficult or stressful, such as with a friend at school or someone at home. See if you can actually feel the anger, disappointment and emotional discomfort in your body. Notice it.

7. Now repeat these words mentally after me:

> This is a moment of challenge.
> This is hurtful. This is stressful.
> I have the strength to stay with this.
> I am not alone.
> Everyone has their own challenges too.
> We all struggle in life.
> But we are OK and I am OK.

8. Now put your right hand on your chest and your left hand on your belly and say these words mentally:

> May I be kind to myself
> May I accept myself as I am
> May I forgive myself
> May I be strong
> May I be happy

9. Notice the sensations and feelings that arise in your body. Sit with them for a few moments until we end the practice. (End the practice in 1–2 minutes.)

10. When you're ready, open your eyes and continue the rest of the day being kind to yourself and others.

CHAPTER 7

How Can My Wisdom Transform into Action?

ere Part II, we will turn our attention to how the wisdom of mindfulness can influence our actions through specific activities. Through these readings and activities, we are going to share with you how the wisdom of mindfulness looks like, feels like and sounds like. These behavioural shifts through the insights and activities can help you achieve wholesomeness in your family.

There are a total of 30 readings in this chapter, and each one comes with an activity for you to experiment with. We encourage you to continue your daily mindfulness practices introduced at the end of each chapter while experimenting with these activities.

We would like you to keep an open mind while doing these readings and experiments. The reason we call them experiments is so you will approach them with the curiosity of a child, not knowing what may happen as a result, without striving to achieve it. This attitude unburdens you of the expectation of specific results and allows you to accept whatever the experience brings out. Some activities may bring joy, laughter and excitement, while some may bring regret, boredom or remorse. Accept all of them with equanimity while you keep your mindfulness practices consistent.

Do feel free to adapt and customise the activities for your children where you feel necessary as you would know your children best.

1. Disciplining Oneself Before Disciplining Your Child

'Be the change that you wish to see in the world.' – Mahatma Gandhi

A mother approached Mahatma Gandhi and told him that her son ate too much sugar and asked him to advise her son to reduce his sugar consumption. Gandhi after reflecting a bit told her to return in two weeks. The mother went away perplexed. Nevertheless, with trust she returned in two weeks with her son. And then Gandhi told the boy to stop eating sugar, emphasising that it was bad for his health. The son promised to do so. The mother was pleased but nevertheless asked Gandhi the reason for the two-week wait. Gandhi responded that he had to first cut back on his own sugar intake, because two weeks ago he had an obsession with it too.

Before you tell your child to focus on their schoolwork, it is better if you do some work with them. We have encountered parents who do not have the habit of reading but expect that their children read more. It is important that we are able to do what we expect of our children before we put expectations on them.

Of course, there are some things that we may expose our children to even though we haven't personally experienced them. You may never have played soccer or danced ballet but that doesn't mean that you need to deprive your children of these experiences.

We are referring more to the concept of role-modelling the values that we hold dear. If we keep giving excuses not to exercise, how do we expect our children to stay committed to any form of sports?

Of course, it is usually easier to give advice than to follow it. I (Kathir) remember a friend telling me his encounter with a doctor who was encouraging him to stop smoking, but it appeared that the doctor was a heavy smoker himself. It is similar to you expecting your child not to get angry but giving yourself the freedom to be so.

Activity 1: Stepping Out of Autopilot

Here is a list of questions to pose to yourself, to examine the habits that are keeping you in autopilot mode. Do this activity yourself first, then, 2–3 weeks later, after you are comfortable with it, try it with your child.

1. What is one habit you would like to change?

2. What maintains this habit?

3. What are the pros and cons of changing this habit?

4a. What do you think is the impact on you?

4b. What do you think is the impact on your child?

4c. In case of your child's habit, how does he feel it impacts his siblings or parents?

5. What is the intention you want to set for yourself regarding this habit?

6. What are some attitudes and mindfulness practices that can help you to realise your intentions? (You can research this on your own.)

7. How will you sustain this change?

2. Learning Together

'Alone we can do so little; together we can do so much.' – Helen Keller

Creating a love of learning rather than making it a chore for your children is an important aspect of wisdom. This requires us to cultivate an *attitude* of learning as opposed to focusing on formal learning.

When I (Kathir) was a young child, my father used to spend time watching documentaries on TV with me. That was how I cultivated curiosity, and I continue to have that with me until today. When this love of learning happens, we are learning all the time. Every experience teaches us. We learn from all directions, from both sentient and insentient beings.

I (Sunita) learnt a lot about compassion, gratitude, resilience and forgiveness from growing up with pets. For example, my pets were full of gratitude every single day when we fed them. One of my dogs, who passed away in 2016, struggled with cancer for more than two years but was always in a good mood regardless of what happened to him.

Learning from daily experiences is perhaps more valuable than formal learning because it then becomes a lifelong attitude. When we have this attitude, we do not see learning as a destination but rather as a journey. Learning becomes a part of living. With this attitude, we are also able to learn better in formal settings, such as at school.

Families can cultivate this learning attitude by sharing what they learned from any experience, however trivial they may seem. We have learned so much from conversations with taxi drivers, professors, street cleaners, CEOs, shopowners and even from nature. We can learn from all directions.

Activity 2: Learning Through Mindful Perception

In this activity, we're going to explore a familiar place using our senses. Include all your family members in this game if you can.

Choose a room in your home where there are many small objects, e.g. furnishings, books, toys. The living room is a good place to try this activity in. See if you can rearrange these objects so as to reduce the familiarity of the place. Ensure that there are no sharp or dangerous objects around.

Now, set a timer for one minute, and everyone closes their eyes and starts walking around the room, with no particular destination in mind. Use your sense of touch to navigate around. When the timer rings, stop wherever you happen to be, and with your eyes still closed, pick up the item closest to you.

Now, from the eldest to the youngest in the family, describe the item in detail based solely on touch and ask the rest to guess what it is. It does not matter if they get it right or wrong. Continue to keep your eyes closed, as the next family member describes the object in as much detail as possible.

Once everyone is done, open your eyes and look at the object that you are holding on to. Look at the packaging, words, shapes and colours. Next, pass your object to the person next to you (in a clockwise direction) and look at the new object you receive. Continue doing this until each family member has seen every object.

Here's a similar activity, but using your sense of hearing this time. As a family, go from room to room and pay attention to the sounds in each space. This could include the sound of the fan, the washing machine or the water running in the kitchen. Name the sounds that you hear. Now, return to the living room, or go to the park, and sit down together in a circle. Sit silently and focus on listening to the sounds near and far. After a minute, share with each other the sounds that you heard.

You can also engage with your sense of smell. Walk around your home and smell as many things as possible within your reach such as your clothes, books, wall, flowers and toys. Notice the differences in the smells. Be curious. They may smell fragrant or neutral or odorous. Just notice each smell.

Explore mindful perception in as many settings as you can. Gradually cultivate this sense of keen perception in your children by asking what they are seeing, smelling, tasting, touching or hearing in any situation.

3. Family Life as a Retreat

'Rejoice with your family in the beautiful land of life.' – Albert Einstein

Jon Kabat-Zinn and Myla Kabat-Zinn compared parenting to being on an 18-year-long retreat. A retreat recharges you and brings great insights about yourself. It's also something that you consciously and voluntarily join. In the same way, parenting and childhood development can be seen as a retreat – a retreat where we practise mindfulness and learn from its insights and create wisdom.

We may presume that everything that happens at a retreat is going to be comfortable and nice. But that is not always the case. I (Kathir) remember being in a retreat where the weather was extremely hot – so hot that I could not sit and reflect on my learnings of the day. There were mosquitoes biting me all the time, which was highly uncomfortable and made me worried about dengue fever. Even the journey to the retreat centre itself was far from relaxing. I had to take a 5-hour flight and then a 3-hour train and finally a 1.5-hour car ride. It was exhausting.

Similarly, family life is not going to be a bed of roses. There will be positive and negative experiences and that is what creates learning. We usually learn and remember better when things get a little uncomfortable and take us out of our comfort zone.

Imagine watching a movie about a man who has a perfect childhood and then he marries the perfect woman and they have the perfect marriage. They raise perfect children and all them become a perfect family. He then becomes a grandparent and spends his life perfectly with his perfect grandchildren. Would you watch such a movie?

Activity 3: Family Shopping Day

Pick a Saturday or Sunday as a family shopping day. Each family member prepares a list of things to buy for the others. You are to buy a maximum of 5 items and a minimum of 2 items. You can choose to define a price range, such as a minimum of $1 and a maximum of $10 per item. Keep your lists secret.

Once the shopping is done and you are back home, sit in a circle and take turns to discuss why each person bought those particular items. For example, if your son bought you a shaver, you might want to understand his reasons. Take it with an attitude of curiosity rather than taking it too literally or as an issue.

4. Me Time

'Knowing how to be solitary is central to the art of loving. When we can be alone, we can be with others without using them as a means of escape.' – Bell Hooks

Not everything needs to be done together with other people. While engagement within the family is very important, it is also important that everyone has sufficient private time on their own to do their own thing. As much as we are relational beings, sometimes too much engagement with others can become a distraction. The mind needs time to engage with itself too.

During these private moments, your mind might trigger questions and ideas that are meaningful to you. It is also during these moments that you might suddenly remember things which you have forgotten for days. 'Me time' opens up an opportunity for your mind to disengage from the usual mode of things and instead engage with things that are truly important to you.

Activity 4: Silent Walk in Nature

Once a week, take a walk in the park, forest or mountains, without listening to any music or talking to anyone. Just be with nature. Observe the birds, butterflies, trees, mountains, hills, and streams – and anything else in your surroundings. After some time, sit on a bench or on the grass and just be with yourself, without the need to do anything. Enjoy your own presence after enjoying the presence of nature.

5. Planning for the Future and Learning from the Past

'Accept the past as the past and realise that each new day you are a new person who doesn't need to carry old baggage into the new day with you.' – Alaric Hutchinson

While being present in the moment and working with such an orientation is very helpful in mindfulness practices, this does not mean that we shouldn't think about the future or the past in our daily lives.

First of all, there are many valuable lessons we can learn from our past. We have all experienced disappointment, but instead of ruminating on it and focusing on the regret or guilt, we should accept the disappointments and focus on the learning behind those experiences. Disappointments tell us a lot about what we value and what we want in life.

With the future, we do not have to be obsessed with it. Instead we can plan for it. Our lessons in life can help us to plan our future in such a way that we can possibly reduce the chances of disappointment.

One interesting thing is that both the life lessons from your past and your plans for your future are taking place in the present moment. The present moment becomes your plane of reference for you to plan your future and learn from the past. Mindfulness helps you to be grounded in the present moment with acceptance so that you can effectively plan what you want in the future.

Similarly, you may have regrets about your parenting, or your child may have regrets about his friendships or school life. Be compassionate to one another and to yourself. The past is in the past. We move forward by learning from it and planning ahead to be more intentional about what we want in the future by focusing on what we can do in the here and now.

Activity 5: Sharing Your Dreams

Here are two images – the first one for your child and the second one for you. Colour the images silently and mindfully. Make conscious choices about the colours you use. Notice how it feels as you go along, including the feeling of the strokes, your thoughts, and your emotions.

Once you have both finished, ask your child questions about her dreams for the future. How might you be able to support her in her dreams? Do not ask her to change her dreams or criticise her dreams. Allow her to explore. You can also share your dreams with her.

Overleaf:
Child's Colouring Sheet (Activity 5)

Overleaf:
Parent's Colouring Sheet (Activity 5)

6. Practise, Practise and Practise

**'For the things we have to learn before we can do them, we learn by doing them.'
– Aristotle**

The foundation of mindful families is practice. There is no mindfulness without practice. Just like learning to cycle, initially it may be a little difficult, but with guidance and practice you will find your balance in no time. That is how it is with mindfulness too.

Mindfulness is a practice you need to sustain. If you do not sustain it, then you may lose it. It is like going to the gym and exercising. When you stop exercising, the muscles will weaken. Mindfulness works in just the same manner. The more you practise, the stronger the 'muscles' stay. Having this understanding in mind helps children and parents make mindfulness part of their life.

Activity 6: Complete the Puzzle

Complete the words below by filling in the missing letters. For example, for _UZZ_E, you need to add the letters P and L to get PUZZLE. Most of the words are related to the attitudes of mindfulness. Try it together with the family, and discuss what the words mean to each of you. We encourage you to practise or be conscious of all of these attitudes daily.

A_ARE_E_S (Noticing fully)

_U_PO_ _ (A sense of direction)

C_N_E_T_D (In sync with someone)

_E_CE_TI_ _ (Part of your senses)

A_ _E_ _A _CE (Inviting all experiences into your life)

_H_NK_ _ L (You feel this when someone does something good for you)

P_TI_ _ CE (You need this in order to complete a difficult task)

CU_ _ _ _ S (Helps you to continually learn)

_OSI_I_E (A feeling when things are going your way)

T_U_ _ (When you can 100% rely on someone or something)

7. Being Comfortable with Silence

'When I pronounce the word Future, the first syllable already belongs to the past. When I pronounce the word Silence, I destroy it.' – Wisława Szymborska

Our minds are naturally prone to speaking as it is the primary mode through which we communicate with others. We assume that speaking is a very important activity for humans, especially seeing that we have invented so many languages and words for this purpose. Silence is therefore seen as something unproductive, useless or to be feared.

Let's think about what silence is. It is simply the absence of verbal activity or sound around you. Verbal activity is usually preceded by thoughts. What silence does, therefore, is to reduce mental activity, allowing you to focus on and pay attention to just your thoughts.

You may have noticed that almost all of the formal mindfulness practices are observed in silence. Silence can be very healthy if we practise it daily. Try being silent for 5 minutes every day without engaging with any device, another person or in any task. This daily practice can be more useful than going for a silent retreat for a prolonged length of time. It is within our daily hustle and bustle that we need to find time for silence.

I (Sunita) remember suggesting to one of my clients at a children's home to sit silently with herself for 2–3 minutes a day. She found the idea strange but was willing to try it out. She had been diagnosed with ADHD and this practice helped her slow her down, freeing her from the need to constantly engage.

One good opportunity for observing mindful silence in your family is to create a deliberate period of silence before the start of a movie or a chat. Even spending some time in silence before having a difficult conversation with your child or asking your child to be silent before a conversation can be very helpful for priming ourselves.

Activity 7: Silent Drawing

All family members are encouraged to partici-pate in this activity. Get yourself a large sheet of paper, e.g. flip-chart paper, or combine four sheets of drawing block paper to form one large piece. Prepare some pencils and colour pencils.

In a fixed sequence, take turns to contribute a single stroke to the sheet of paper. Continue building up the art work for 15 minutes while observing the following rules:

- Everyone has to draw and/or colour using the pencils or colour pencils provided.
- Everyone must contribute to the drawing.
- Everyone must be silent throughout the process. No talking or signalling to one another using gestures.
- Everyone must stop once the timer stops at 15 minutes, regardless of what they were doing.

At the end of the 15 minutes, you could talk about the process as a family, sharing your thoughts and feelings before the activity started, during and after. Or, you could also choose to end the activity once the time is up, without the need to discuss further.

8. Healthy Relationships

'Good relationships are based on kindness.'
– Jane Green

The foundation of healthy relationships is well-being. Family relationships are healthy when everyone understands that the relationships with one another are cherished and nourished on the foundation of well-being. It means that we care for one another and are there to support one another in times of need and celebrate together in moments of joy. We communicate mindfully and with respect. Parents do not pamper the children or favour one child over another. The family also makes time for each other every day where possible, even if it's for 5–10 minutes.

One thing we see happening quite often in families is well-being-centred relationships being replaced or challenged by success-centred relationships. In a success-centred relationship, the family is more interested in achieving their individual goals, and each person's worth is measured by that. The parents are measured by how hard they work for the family's financial comfort. The children's success is measured by their grades and sports achievements.

In no way are we saying that success or grades are not important. Rather, we need to be aware that well-being can be there even without success and grades, and that success and grades don't necessarily bring well-being. Success and grades can certainly help us enhance our well-being, but only if we know how to place them within the grand scheme of our life.

Activity 8: Mindful Conversation

One of the biggest grievances many children have is that their parents don't listen to them, either because they are too busy or because they try to be 'know-it-alls'. Mindful conversations provide an opportunity to change this negative experience to a positive one.

Choose a time in the day when the whole family is able to sit down together. This could be after dinner, for example. If it is too much of a challenge to do it every day due to the family's schedules, then commit to 2–3 times a week to focus on mindful conversations.

The first step in mindful conversations is mindful listening, where you keep an open mind and listen patiently to the person speaking, with the intention of fully understanding them. This applies to every family member.

The second step is to be curious and ask questions. Be non-judgemental when any family member is speaking and focus on the intention. One way to reduce judging is to remind ourselves that there are multiple perspectives and multiple ways to resolve any issue. Remember the intention is to understand one another, not to focus on who is right or wrong or smarter. We are not in a battle but rather in a loving family relationship.

To start the ball rolling, think of at least 10 topics you wish to have a mindful conversation on. Here are some ideas: where to go for a holiday, happiest moments in school today, sharing stories of your children's younger years, dreams, favourite movies, etc. The list is long. Talk about things that as a family, you are genuinely interested in.

9. From Complaining to Contribution

'Every thought, every word, and every action that adds to the positive and the wholesome is a contribution to peace. Each and every one of us is capable of making such a contribution.' – Aung San Suu Kyi

We often complain when we are dissatisfied with something. It could be a meal at a restaurant that tasted bad, or service that was not delivered in line with your expectations, or your spouse or child not listening to you in conversation.

One aspect of complaints is the locus of control, which is basically how much control we have over the situation. For example, you have some control over a situation where a salesman did not serve you professionally, in that you could request for another staff member to serve you, or just walk over to another shop. However, if the weather spoiled your plans for a day out with your family, there's less that you can control, because you cannot change the weather. Nevertheless, you could still manage the situation by having a Plan B, such as playing games indoors. Complaining about either of these situations will not change anything. And yet we complain.

Why do we complain? There are a variety of reasons, from wanting to vent, wanting to connect with another person or wanting to get attention, to simply being a chronic complainer. Chronic complaining is a difficult habit to change unless self-awareness is raised. Chronic complainers do not know that they are constantly complaining, and this can become a culture in your family if you are not aware of it.

People who need to vent are usually looking for validation, attention and/or sympathy. They are not interested in solutions or advice. They may feel better after venting although no solutions are reached. There is research that suggests that mindfulness can reduce such frustrations and also reduce the complaining behaviour.

Let us explore what we can do instead of complaining.

Think about what you can contribute in any situation that you are dissatisfied with. If your child complains about something, listen to him and allow him to vent for a few minutes. Empathise with him and allow him enough space and time to say all that he wants to say. Once he has calmed down and you have heard him out, invite him to experiment with you on a different way of processing his feelings. Ask him what he can do about the situation. What change can he bring to the situation? If he is unable to think of a way to contribute, encourage him to think of the smallest possible step forward. If that too is not possible, thank him for trying and focus instead on internal change, i.e. acceptance and perhaps a lesson learned about himself and others. If, however, he has thought of a way to make a change to the situation, support him by offering to help him with the step forward.

Activity 9: Contributing to Society

This activity is to be done with your child. Here are two images, the first one for your child and the second one for you. Colour the images silently and mindfully. Make conscious choices about the colours you use, and notice your bodily sensations, thoughts and emotions as you go along.

Once you have both finished, ask your child what the two images are telling us. You can steer the conversation to the point about how she can be that missing piece that makes the image complete. Similarly ask her how she can contribute to the family and society. Inquire into details such as how she would feel if she did these acts, how it helps others, what she thinks about, and other questions. Also ask her how she can do this more often or if she can think of new ways of contributing to the world and how you could support her.

Be genuinely curious. You can also share what you are doing to contribute to the family, the community, and the world.

Overleaf:
Child's Colouring Sheet (Activity 9)

Contribution

Overleaf:
Parent's Colouring Sheet (Activity 9)

10. Mindful Discipline

'Do not train a child to learn by force or harshness; but direct them to it by what amuses their minds, so that you may be better able to discover with accuracy the peculiar bent of the genius of each.' – Plato

Often children are punished for wrongdoings and rewarded for the opposite. In these methods, apart from becoming compliant, children do not learn the value of doing the right thing. Moreover, most disciplinary actions do not take into account the child's emotional dimension. A lot of the questions that parents use to 'interrogate' their children seem to be aimed at proving the child's guilt, with little or no intention for the child to learn. Punishment is simply used as a deterrent.

The mindfulness way of disciplining children involves the psychology of the child and what good she can do to repair the wrong or the harm done. It is based on compassion and self-awareness, and it is wrongdoing-centred instead of wrongdoer-centred. There is a clear separation of the person from the problem without denying the connection between the two.

We have created a conversation script, integrating mindfulness and restorative practices, that will allow parents to discipline their children mindfully. You can try this script whenever your child has done something wrong. Please ensure that your child has admitted to the wrongdoing before using the following script because the script does not work with a child who has not admitted to the wrongdoing. Also, take time to calm yourself for the conversation through short mindfulness practices if necessary.

Activity 10: Mindful Discipline Script

This script is to be used by the parent to guide the child when something wrong has happened in the family or outside the family. Feel free to adapt the script based on the maturity of your child but do keep to the intention of each of the statements.

1. Sit down or stand when doing this practice.

2. Close your eyes.

3. Notice your body weight on the chair or the floor.

4. Take a minute or two to notice your breath as you inhale and exhale naturally.

5. Now that you have admitted to the wrongdoing, what emotions are you feeling?

6. Take note of this emotion. And accept this emotion without the need to reject it. It is fine to feel this way. Stay with these emotions.

7. Now, notice what is happening in your body. Notice all the sensations and stay with it.

8. Now open your eyes and let's have a conversation. I want to understand what happened and how I can help you to move forward.

- With regards to the wrongdoing, please tell me what happened?
- What were you thinking at that time?
- What have you thought about since?
- Who has been affected by what you did?
- What can you do to make things right?
- What can I do to help you?
- What shall be our first step?

9. Thank you for having this conversation with me.

10. Let's take a minute to now practise the Coping Breathing Space together (refer to the script on Coping Breathing Space).

11. Labelling Emotions and Responding

'Between stimulus and response there is a space. In that space is our power to choose our response. In our response lies our growth and our freedom.' – Viktor Frankl

One of the first things that helps in difficult conversations is labelling our emotions. We may think that an emotion rising within us is unknown to others but it is common for people we are talking to to sense our discomfort although they may not know exactly what that emotion is.

Therefore, it is important that we communicate the emotion we are feeling in any given moment, whether it is favourable or unfavourable. For example, 'I am feeling very upset right now with the news that you have just given me.' Or 'I feel so happy right now. Your promotion is well deserved for the hard work that you put in in the last 18 months.'

Labelling our emotions when we speak to others can help others understand us and our actions better. Children learn this from their parents. Here is an illustration from a child's perspective.

The child's father comes home after spending the evening out with his friends. He was supposed to buy groceries, but he forgot. The mother gets angry and accuses him of valuing his friends over the family. She raises her voice and an argument ensues, with each blaming the other. From one corner, the child is watching the entire episode, frightened by the exchange of harsh words.

What does the child learn from this incident? She learns that when you are angry, you can state your opinions, raise your voice and say things to win the argument regardless of whether you are right or wrong. If this happens often enough, the child learns a new behaviour. In future, when she feels that her needs are not met, she will do exactly the same. This is one of the ways children learn to validate and legitimise their responses to unwholesome emotions.

I (Sunita) was conducting a parenting talk a couple of years back and one of the parents in the hall asked how to change a negative behaviour in her son. Her son would slam the car door whenever he was angry with her and refused to listen to her not to take his anger out on the car. After we had a short conversation, she realised that her son had learned the behaviour from her, as she too slammed the house door and car door when she was angry with her business associates. We discussed ways to first change our own behaviours if we want our children to change their behaviours.

Let's re-create the story above from a wisdom perspective. The father comes home after spending the evening out with his friends. He was supposed to buy groceries, but he forgot. The mother gets angry, and she tells him that she is feeling angry because he forgot to buy the groceries as he had promised just 3 hours earlier. She waits for a few seconds to calm herself before asking with a calm voice and genuine curiosity. The father accepts responsibility for his actions and admits that he forgot while he was having fun. He apologises and offers to immediately step out and buy the groceries. She accepts his apology and asks him to get it the next day instead of rushing out. She also suggests that he find ways to help himself remember in future. He agrees.

Here, the child learns that it is fine to be upset or angry and that a calm conversation can still take place instead of shouting and arguing. The child also learns about responsibility, forgiveness and moving to solutions rather than fault-finding. She learns that she too can respond to changing situations in the same way.

Activity 11: Thoughts and Feelings Exercise

We recommend that you first practise this activity on yourself before exploring it with your child. Think of a situation where you have positive or negative emotions and write it in the table below, together with your thoughts and feelings. What do you notice? What is causing you to feel upset or disappointed? Is it the situation or is it your thoughts?

Situation	Thoughts	Feelings / Emotions
Example: My colleague didn't join me for lunch for two consecutive days and she went out with another group. She didn't even inform me and we lunch together everyday.	She is upset with me about something. She is moving away from me. She doesn't like me anymore.	Disappointed, sad, angry, confused

Now, sit down with your child and think of a variety of situations, and your child's thoughts and feelings about each of them. Help him label the emotions if he is not able to, for instance by using emoji or pictures of children showing a variety of facial expressions.

After this practice, help your child see how his thoughts impact his emotions. Mindfulness practices help us in the area of our thoughts and interpretations so that our emotions do not spiral downwards.

Situation	Thoughts	Feelings / Emotions
Example: My friend Susan didn't smile at me in school today.	She is ignoring me on purpose. She doesn't like me. She is proud.	Sad, angry

12. Do's and Don'ts

'Words are, of course, the most powerful drug used by mankind.' – Rudyard Kipling

The words 'Do' and 'Don't' impact the brain differently. Here's an example:

Don't make that noise.
vs
Allow me to listen. The noise is distracting me from focusing on my meeting. Please lower your volume.

In the first case, while you might say 'Don't make that noise' with the right intentions, your child only hears a restraining instruction. She doesn't get to understand why she should stop making that noise. The second statement, in contrast, helps your child to appreciate the value of the change that is required and what change is needed. This approach works when you want your child to process what is being said rather than just follow your instructions. It is useful when what is to be learned is important but not urgent or an emergency.

Don't touch that, it's hot.
vs
The object is hot. Stay away from it as you might get burnt.

In this situation, 'Don't touch that, it's hot', is also a restraining instruction. The word 'Don't' has the desired effect of getting the person's attention immediately. 'Don't' is very useful when used in emergencies as it triggers the amygdala in the brain to react fast. However, we also want children to learn why they should not touch any hot object, not just this specific object. Unless it is an emergency, we can express the statement without using 'Don't'.

Replacing these words can improve relationships in the family because it allows the other person to learn what is important and what requires their immediate action.

Activity 12: Spot the Differences

As a family, look at the two following pictures and spot the differences between them by paying attention to every detail.

When you are done, discuss what the words 'Just be' mean to each of you. We all spend too much time doing or not doing things. What would it be like to just be in the present moment? You might have heard people saying, 'Don't just sit there, do something.' We are constantly doing one thing or other, and we might even feel guilty when we have nothing to do. Perhaps it is okay to just be. Explore what happens when you just sit, close your eyes and focus on listening to your body or just appreciating your breath as it flows in and out of your body.

You may choose to end the activity by colouring the pictures silently and mindfully.

Overleaf:
**Spot the Differences and
Child's Colouring Sheet (Activity 12)**

Overleaf:

**Spot the Differences and
Parent's Colouring Sheet (Activity 12)**

13. Noticing Our Default Reaction

'We first make our habits, then our habits make us.' – John Dryden

All of us have a default reaction when we find ourselves in an unfavourable situation, such as in a crisis or when we are highly stressed. These are usually emotions that are unwholesome. And unwholesome emotions usually have a negative behavioural effect.

One of my (Sunita) clients who was looking for an intimate relationship shared how she was having a really tough time. Every time she met someone, she found that they did not want to pursue the relationship beyond the second date. In our sessions, I realised that in her dinner date conversations, she tended to express her disagreement very quickly, even on lighthearted topics. Her default reaction was to challenge her dates' assumptions. This put them off as they did not want to struggle in a conversation with someone they were meeting for just the second time. She would get even more annoyed with them for refusing to engage. And because they didn't call her for a third date, she would feel rejected and regretful. And yet, with the next date, the behaviour would repeat itself.

We could express the default chain reaction in this situation as follows:

Issue → Disagreement → Non-engagement/ engagement → Annoyance → Rejection → Regret

In a similar way, all of us have our default emotions. In mindfulness, we do not reject any of these emotions, whether positive or negative. Instead, the intention is to observe the thoughts and emotions and the corresponding actions and effects.

How can you apply this in your family? You can start by noticing what types of emotions rise in situations where your child may not have met your expectations or did something wrong. Notice the emotion and stay with it without rejecting or judging it. It is just an emotion. By accepting the emotion as it is, you will be able to slowly change the reactive nature of the emotion to something more neutral, such as calmness or tranquillity. Very often, we try to escape or ignore or fight against emotions that are difficult. Just stay with the emotion.

Also note that it is not just your emotion and its effects that matter in creating a mindful family. The chain reaction extends into the emotions of your family members as well.

Suppose you are trembling with fear due to some bad news you received and are unable to talk for some time. You need your own space at this point. Your child asks you a question and you are too trapped in your emotions to respond. Your child may feel annoyed at this if she does not know why you are feeling the way you do. She feels angry that you are not answering her question and raises her voice. She tells you off and slams her door on you when you do turn around to explain yourself. As a result, you may feel sad or angry that your child has become unruly and disobedient and not understanding of your situation. This might then perhaps result in you crying and wondering where you went wrong in parenting.

This scenario clearly shows that our emotions impact the emotions of other people. Usually, positive emotions create positive emotions in others, and negative ones create a negative chain reaction. This is why when we see someone smile at us, we easily smile back at them and feel good about each other.

It is therefore important that we are aware of our default reactions. Seek to understand the other person before making any conclusions. The last word does not always have to be yours when you see a negative emotion rising in your awareness. Let it be. Let it go.

Activity 13: Noticing your Thoughts and Feelings

Here are two images, the first one for your child and the second one for you. For your child's image, ask him or her to first complete the person's face with eyes, mouth, hairstyle, etc. After that, both of you can begin to colour your images silently and mindfully. As before, make conscious choices about the colours you pick and notice your sensations, thoughts and emotions as you are colouring.

Once you have both finished, ask your child what she was thinking about before she started drawing and colouring as well as when she was colouring. Explore if the thoughts were positive, negative or neutral. How did

these thoughts make her feel? Talk about your own thoughts and feelings too.

Next, sit silently for 1–2 minutes, using a timer to set an alarm. Observe the thoughts that arise as you are seated, noticing each one without trying to change it or reject it. After the alarm rings, you can discuss what types of thoughts kept coming up. And what were some feelings that were arising with these thoughts?

Do this practice whenever you can, and see what insights you get about your child's thoughts and feelings.

Notice Your Thoughts

Overleaf:
Child's Colouring Sheet (Activity 13)

Notice Your Thoughts

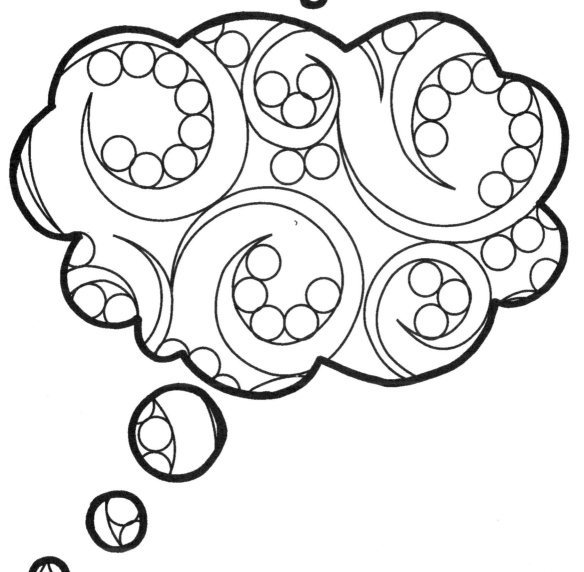

Overleaf:
Parent's Colouring Sheet (Activity 13)

14. Balancing Self-Gratitude with Pro-Social Gratitude

'Let us be grateful to the people who make us happy; they are the charming gardeners who make our souls blossom.' – Marcel Proust

Research on gratitude suggests that it can improve mental health, relationships, empathy and self-esteem. With gratitude, we acknowledge what we already have within and among us that we usually do not notice or perhaps only notice occasionally.

We have a built-in negative bias in our brains, which comes from our primitive days when were always on the alert for predators. We carry this instinct in our brains even now, when we are on the lookout for what could harm us in our surroundings. However, being on constant alert can also tire us out, and we may miss moments to be grateful for the simple of things in life.

When you express gratitude, your brain releases more dopamine and serotonin. You feel happier, less fearful and anxious, and over time you become healthier too. You start to notice things you took for granted, such as your sane mind, wisdom, good-natured children, supportive and hardworking spouse, beautiful home, safe country, and much else besides.

What else can you think of to be grateful for, in this very moment?

While it is perfectly fine to focus on self-gratitude, we encourage mindful families to also practise gratitude for self and others. As a family, record the things that you are grateful for which came from the efforts of others beyond the immediate family members. This could be the janitor who keeps the toilets clean at your workplace or school, the security guard who keeps the compound safe, the drivers on the road who drive in an orderly manner so that you can all safely return to your family, or your children's teachers who go out of their way to help your child progress in their education.

This is called pro-social gratitude, where we are thankful for things that were not caused by ourselves. By doing this exercise daily as a family, we become more pro-social, less self-centred and more connected to one another.

Activity 14a: Gratitude Tree

Start a family gratitude tree. Draw a tree on a large sheet of paper and put it up on a wall somewhere in the house. Every day, before going to bed, sit down as a family (or individually) and write down what you are grateful for in the day on a sheet of note paper and paste it on the tree. We recommend writing 1–3 grateful notes per day.

After a month or so, go through all the notes as a family, or each member can do it on their own time – whatever works for your family.

If your children prefer journalling in a book or in an app, or putting their notes in a gratitude jar, that's all fine too. The idea is to do it consistently.

Activity 14b: Gratitude Card

In this activity, we'd like everyone to write a 'thank you' card to each family member. Perhaps as parents, you could get the ball rolling. You can either buy or make a card. Write at least 3 things you are grateful to that family member for. Describe what you mean in as much detail as possible. Send the card to the recipient by mail if you like! There is something magical about receiving positive notes, especially when it is unexpected.

15. Supportive Attitude

'Strong people don't put others down... They lift them up.' – Michael P. Watson

Supporting each other when in need is a great way for family bonds to be strengthened. This includes going out of your way to help each other even when no one asks for it. It is about being aware of and sensitive to each other's needs. Cultivating this supportive attitude early in your child's life is very important.

There is a common belief in most families that older siblings should help and support the younger ones. This can become a burden on the older child. Instead, we recommend that support and help should be rendered not by the age of the child but rather each child doing and giving what they can.

We can encourage children to help their parents when in need. And always acknowledge their contributions. Helping each other in chores when asked is good but teaching children to help each other even when not asked can be especially meaningful. Children grow up knowing that they are positive contributors to one another as a family and even in society.

Beyond helping each other, you can also support each other by being there for family members emotionally, especially during challenging times. This bond remains in place through your children's adult years and in their relationships with their spouse and children.

We can teach children that sometimes all that is needed is to be able to sit with their siblings or parents when feeling down. Simple acts like this go to show that we are expressing these acts from a place of compassion, empathy and kindness.

Activity 15: Exchanging Roles

For this activity, choose a weekend where everyone will be home. Agree the night before that you will all exchange roles for the whole of the following day. You could also explore exchanging roles for specific tasks, or for just 1 or 2 hours instead, if your children are very young.

The rule is that the day has to function exactly like a typical Saturday or Sunday so that the family still functions well. So, for example, the child gets to play the role of the parent and has to ensure that everything that needs to be done for the day is done. If there are two or more children, they'll need to negotiate the day's activities. They can ask the adults for help on things they can't do, such as the cooking. If the mother or father is usually the one who reminds the child to study, then for this day, the child has to remind both his parents to start studying, and the parents have to study something at that allocated hour.

Plan it in a way that works for your family. The idea is that you should experience a few hours of what it feels like to be in each other's shoes.

At the end of the day, sit down as a family and talk about the entire day's experience. Be compassionate about your observations and don't judge one another. Discuss some of the challenges you faced and what you learned from this experience. Be willing to offer or ask for support in any areas for the future.

16. Earning Trust

'In the end, you have to choose whether or not to trust someone.' – Sophie Kinsella

Families need to build trust in order to flourish. In fact, trust is one of the first things we learn as a child. We trusted our parents and caregivers when they fed us milk and food, held us to comfort us when we were fearful and did all they could to nurture our growth and development. This trust, or the lack of it, can become subconscious as we grow older.

Trust is built two-ways. We need to trust others for others to trust us. We cannot expect people to always trust us if we make no effort to trust them. There are five ways to develop trust, which are embedded within the word itself:

T - Truth
R - Reliability
U - Understanding
S - Sincerity
T - Transparency

We need to value **truth**. We need to speak the truth in front of children and others alike. This should be consistent and done all the time, except in exceptional situations where someone's life may be in danger. If you have not been consistently valuing truth, it is not too late. Start now and stay committed to it.

Reliability is measured against time. It is related to the consistency with which parents behave in various situations as well as the predictable nature of the parents. Parents who keep changing their minds or behaviour make it difficult for their children to understand them. The child grows up feeling that her parents cannot be trusted or are unreliable. The predictability of your behaviour is crucial in building trust.

Parents need to make an effort to foster **understanding** with their children. Listen to your children to try and appreciate their perspectives. They will feel more connected to you, less judged and more willing to come to you to talk about their challenges and jointly think of solutions. Open communication about anything and everything deepens understanding within the family.

I (Sunita) conduct courses on relationships in tertiary institutions for students aged 18 to 19. On the topic of sexual relationships, 80-90% of the students said that their parents would not be able to talk to them about it. Some shared that their parents would either avoid the topic or tell them not to have sex rather than having a conversation about it. For those whose parents who could speak to them about sex without awkwardness, there was already a strong relationship and open communication in place. One student said that she could talk to both of her parents about anything that was bothering her, including problems with her boyfriend. They always listened to her and would sometimes share some of their own challenges. She felt that since her parents' relationship was not perfect either, she should not expect that in her own relationship.

When parents make the effort to understand their children, their children too make the effort to understand them and others. It takes a lot of time and patience, but the rewards are more than worth it.

Children can sense our **sincerity**. Sincerity is defined as being genuine and honest. Telling your children that they are on the right path when they are not, or being silent when things are not heading in the right direction, is the opposite of sincerity. Parents need to be sincere even when dealing with hard truths. Spend time listening to your child's point of view with the intention of understanding his views and challenges before helping him to see why things need to be done differently, if necessary.

Transparency and openness are also required in building trust. Parents need to be willing to disclose what they are feeling and thinking where and when appropriate. Of course, discretion is required when it comes to transparency. Being too open or not managing boundaries would not be helpful to a very young child who is unable to comprehend what is happening. Transparency has to be age-appropriate.

One of my (Kathir) students said that his father had shared with him that he had cheated in school exams in his younger days. The father seemed proud of the fact that he had gotten away with it. The father had shared this when the boy was just 10 years old, when he was caught cheating on a test. His father scolded him for being caught. Instead of helping his child see the reason why cheating is not acceptable, the father did an inappropriate self-disclosure and encouraged the wrong behaviour. Transparency and openness come with responsibility.

Without trust, we shake the very fundamental experience of human beings right from infancy. Trust is therefore absolutely essential in mindful families.

Activity 16: Family Tree

Part of creating trust in a family is knowing the family tree – the history of the family and the connections within. We encourage you to create a family tree of at least three generations and share as many insights about each person in the family as possible.

Draw the family tree together with your children on a large piece of paper. You might need two or more sheets of flip-chart paper depending on the size of your family. You can also choose to do this online using family tree generators.

Once done, find a photograph of each family member when they were young (preferably under 7 years old) as well as a recent photo of them, and paste them on the tree side by side. This includes members of the family who have passed on. If you are unable to find any, that's OK, you can leave it blank.

Once the family tree is done, you may wish to write down three things that you appreciate about each person or something unique about them. You can add as many things as you like. You can also share your stories of each person, e.g. how they impacted you.

Hang your family tree somewhere in your home where you can see it often and reflect on the relationships. You may add more things to the tree over time, especially when new members join the family.

17. Being a Human 'Being'

'Man is the only creature who refuses to be what he is.' – Albert Camus

What do you think about when you have free time? If your weekend were to be free, what would you do? For most of us, we are always looking for something to 'do'. We make plans to do things, whether by ourselves or as a family. It could be watching a movie, going out for a picnic or having a party at home. What does this tell us about our nature?

Although we are human beings, we have somehow become human 'doings'. Our minds are automatically inclined to find something to do. There are many reasons for this tendency.

The first is that our sensory organs are naturally drawn to the external world of sensory engagement. You notice this phenomenon even with toddlers. Toddlers venture into the world by reaching out and crawling, as they want to feel, taste and listen to what's around them. This behaviour endures into adulthood.

Another reason is that we often associate doing things with productivity. Actions produce results and therefore when you are sitting and doing nothing, you assume that it is not productive because nothing is created.

However, in mindfulness, apart from doing, we also need time for being. We can define being as an inward journey, as compared to doing, which takes you into the external world. In mindfulness practices, we direct the flow of our energy inwards. Even reading a book about your true nature and reflecting on it is being with yourself.

Activity 17: Being with Oneself

Try this out as a family. Have each person in the family go into a different room or some space in the home where they can be alone. Sit alone on the bed or sofa or the floor without doing anything. Agree as a family on how long you will sit silently (we recommend 10–20 minutes), and set an alarm. Do not use your phone or read or watch a movie or anything. Just sit there silently. You may keep your eyes open or closed.

When the time is up, write down your answers to the following questions. Take about 10 minutes to do this:

- What were some of your thoughts before you started this practice?
- What were some repeated thoughts that arose as you sat there?

- Were you bored? How did that feel?
- What were some of your urges as you sat there?
- What were some emotions coming up as you sat there?
- How did you feel when the alarm rang? Were you relieved?
- How willing are you to do this daily? Why?

Once everyone is done and if you would like to, have a conversation about your experience. Remember not to judge each other in the process. Just mindfully listen to each other's experiences with a sense of curiosity.

Encourage each other to explore 5–10 minutes or more of silent time weekly to just be with oneself.

18. Focusing on What Is Working

'Mind is a flexible mirror, adjust it, to see a better world.' – Amit Ray

Our minds are naturally drawn towards the negative as a protective mechanism to ensure our safety. As a result, we are constantly looking out for imperfections around us. This could be the environment we are in, the people we work or live with, the situations that we are put in or the policies that we are subjected to.

This negative bias creates a language of fault-finding in our heads. We have often seen parents tell their child things like 'Can't you do this right?' or 'This is such an easy task, and you are taking such a long time.' These statements imply that the child is incapable or incompetent. It belittles the child. Sometimes we do not mean to be condescending, but it comes out subconsciously.

So what we can learn to do with mindfulness training? Look at what is right and what is working in your life on a daily basis. This could include the joyful children that you have, your understanding spouse, or your supportive colleagues. Are you noticing and focusing on the great things that your children are doing? It could be the fact that your child is now learning to play soccer well or he has helped someone in need. These are the things that are working well. Focus on these more often, and you'll be able to rewire your brain.

Activity 18: Write a Poem

This is a collective family poem, and the subject is your family and your lives. We suggest focusing on what is going well in your family.

To start, get everyone together to first write down all the key moments or actions that your family considers to be working well. Now, use these good moments to start writing the poem. To challenge yourself, try to write a poem that is at least 100 words.

Once the poem has been composed, choose one member of the family to read it out loud to the whole family as if you are at a poetry recital. After this reading, you can make any changes you like to create a final poem.

The poem should sound positive and pleasant, and it should excite everyone. Hang your family's masterpiece somewhere in the home so that everyone has access to it.

19. Non-Judgemental Vision

'People almost invariably arrive at their beliefs not on the basis of proof but on the basis of what they find attractive.' – Blaise Pascal

Non-judgement is about accepting any experience that arises during our mindfulness practices. Being non-judgemental also means that we should try to move from subjectivity to objectivity when making judgements.

By subjectivity, we are referring to our evaluations and assessments of people and situations through our lenses of values, likes, dislikes, beliefs and opinions. In contrast, by being objective, we evaluate things based on information and data. We see things as they are. As you practise mindfulness, you start looking at things more objectively. That said, there is also space for subjectivity. This is where you bring fun and joy into your life.

One thing to note: The non-judgement that we observe in mindfulness practices need not always be extended to our daily lives. This is not pragmatic. In our daily lives, there are many evaluations and judgements that we have to make. For example, if you are driving and you reach a traffic junction to make a right turn, you need to make a judgement about when to turn based on the oncoming traffic. In business discussions, you need to make decisions that will steer the project to a successful conclusion.

Activity 19: Being Non-judgemental

Here are two images here, one for your child and one for you. You'll notice that the child's image is slanted and has a line running through it. This was done with the intention to encourage accepting its non-perfection.

For this colouring activity, choose two colours for your child to use. She has no choice over the colours. For yourself, however, you can use all the colours that you want. Your child is not allowed to share your colours.

Set a timer for 5 minutes and start colouring. At the end of 5 minutes, both of you should stop colouring, even if you're not done. Ask your child the following questions:

- How do you feel about the colours that were given to you?

- How do you feel about me having so many options of colours when you did not? Is it fair?
- Do you like or dislike the colours?
- Why do you think I only gave you two colours? Do you think I had a choice? Do you always have choices in life?
- What were moments in your life when you felt that you were unfairly treated? What happened? How did you feel? What were your thoughts? How did you react? How did you cope? What could be an alternative way of looking at the same episode?

Now resume colouring. Your child can now use all the colours that she wants with no restrictions.

Non-
Judgement

Overleaf:
Child's Colouring Sheet (Activity 19)

Non-Judgement

Overleaf:
Parent's Colouring Sheet (Activity 19)

20. The Roles We Play

'I took on the shape of a girl.' – Emma Cline

One of the insights we get from mindfulness practices is that while we play many roles in life, we are not the roles.

What does that mean? Let's assume that you are Timothy. Timothy is a son to one person, a husband to another, an employee to an organisation, and a father to his daughter. Each of these roles has a distinct set of responsibilities. But they do not define Timothy, although he may choose one role over the other depending on how much he has invested in that role.

A role that we have invested in more tends to take up more of our time and energy. Perhaps some of our roles give us more satisfaction than others. For example, the CEO of a company would probably find it difficult to let go of her role when she is at home because she is connected to the CEO role 24/7. However, when the CEO gets home at the end of the day, technically the role ends, and other roles such as being a spouse or mother take centrestage. Are we able to let go of our favourite roles or the roles in which we have invested the most?

Most of our conflicts arise when two roles collide. The role of being a parent, when carried to the workplace, could give rise to conflicts with the role of being an employee. Therefore, we need to be very clear of our roles and responsibilities in a given situation. Mindfulness allows you to have that clarity even in such conflicting situations.

Eventually, you will start seeing that you are actually none of these roles. All of these roles have a birth date and an expiry date. These were roles that you picked up along the way and some were roles given to you. Through all of these roles, you remain fundamentally a simple human being wanting happiness. It is this human being that has taken on the role of mother, employee, wife, daughter, etc. The human being can also exist without any of these roles. Just as you have taken up various roles in time, the roles can also end at some point in time. It is like clothes that are worn out. You throw away the torn clothes and replace them with new ones. The same applies to your roles. We need not be overly attached to any of these roles. You seldom see people fighting over their torn clothes as if they were treasure.

Stay anchored on this fact, and soon you will find that the roles you play cannot bind you anymore, because they are relative and not absolute.

Activity 20: Your Roles

Write down all the roles that you play in life. Then list the things that you like and dislike about each role, how much time you invest in them and whether the role energises you or depletes your energy.

Then, reflect on some or all of these questions:

- Which role do you think is your favourite?
- Which role do you always avoid or avoid at times?
- Which role seems to dominate your current life?

- If you could remove one role, which would it be? Why would you remove this role?
- Which role would you like to have more time for? What would you do differently if you had more time in this role?

You may wish to do a simpler version of this activity with your children. You could ask them to write down the roles they play and what they like and dislike about each one. Depending on the age of the child, you can expand further to include the reflection questions.

Role	Likes	Dislikes	Time invested	Is it energising?

21. The Amygdala Strikes Back

**'When you react, you let others control you. When you respond, you are in control.'
– Bohdi Sanders**

Once, when I (Kathir) was at a shopping mall, I heard a loud voice and a child crying. A mother was screaming at her son because of a misdemeanour on his part. The boy was possibly 8 or 9 years old. He was frozen in terror and could only cry as his mother raised her voice at him. This is the freeze reaction of the brain. The moment the child freezes, the amygdala is now overactive, and the child is unable to activate the pre-frontal cortex to think rationally or make objective decisions. Instead, he is consumed by fear. The amygdala has hijacked his brain.

What happens when our amygdala is hijacked? There are three possible reactions: we could either fight back, take flight or freeze. When children start arguing and defending themselves in a situation, then the fight reaction is now active. If unchecked, it will escalate into more violent behaviours. The flight reaction is when the child wants to run away from you. They feel threatened in the situation and thus devise ways to escape. You can notice the restlessness in them when the flight reaction is activated. Freezing happens when the child does not fight or run away but instead stands there looking shocked, crying or even peeing in their pants.

We encourage you to think about your conscious and unconscious behaviours that could be triggering your child's amygdala. This may happen when you exert your power, or when you insist on one way of doing things, or when you hit or restrain them against their wishes. Such behaviours trigger the child's amygdala, thereby not allowing them to learn from the situation. When a child is fearful, he is simply not able to learn.

For example, if your child does not understand a math problem, instead of scolding her for not focusing (which would trigger the amygdala), ask her to take a break and come back after 10 minutes to the same problem or to approach you or her teacher for help. If the child feels overwhelmed and is unable to think, take a pause and practise mindfulness for 5–10 minutes. Mindfulness tames the amygdala while activating and engaging the pre-frontal cortex.

Activity 21: Write a Song

This is a collective family activity. Pick a song that the whole family likes. Print out the lyrics and sing together as a family. Take some time to then analyse the lyrics together. What do you notice about the choice of words? What do you think were the emotions of the lyricist?

Now, create a song that uplifts your family. You can either create one song together, or each family member can create their own song, since you may have different tastes in music. You could take an existing song and write your own lyrics. Be creative and flexible. The song doesn't have to be long, but it should be motivating and catchy.

Next, if each member of the family created their own song, invite them to sing the song in front of everyone else. No comments should be made by any family member except to show encouragement either in actions or words. If you wrote one family song instead of individual songs, you can sing together and perhaps even record it.

22. Being Compassionate, Kind and Empathetic

'No one has ever become poor by giving.'
– **Anne Frank**

Compassion is the feeling that we experience when we are conscious of the pain and suffering of others and wish to help them through various means. Empathy is the rationalisation of what it would be like to be in that person's shoes. Compassion and empathy make us truly human, and expressing it inspires others, creating a ripple effect.

Compassion and empathy in families allow us to be sensitive to each other's pain. This promotes greater understanding among family members if they are going through challenging situations. We provide a listening ear rather than adding to their challenges. In our daily busyness, we tend not to notice the pain of others and sometimes even inflict greater pain on them. This is not done with any bad intentions but simply out of lack of awareness.

Who is most compassionate or empathetic in your family? How did he or she become compassionate or empathetic? These questions can trigger great insights.

Our response due to the feeling of compassion or empathy is kindness. Kindness is an act that allows you to alleviate someone's suffering or distress. Researchers have found that kindness is a universal value across global cultures and time. What are some acts of kindness that you have noticed in your family? What else could you do as a family?

Be kind to everyone, especially to your family members. This isn't as easy as it sounds, because familiarity breeds contempt. The more familiar we are with someone, the harder it is to be compassionate towards them. Perhaps it's because we take the person for granted.

You may also find that you are prone to being selective about who you want to be empathetic towards. This is called selective empathy. Be aware of this tendency without any judgement.

The triangle of humanity, the idea of being human, includes being compassionate, having empathy and doing acts of kindness.

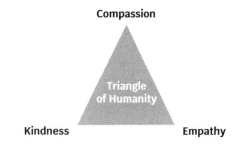

Activity 22: Compassion

This activity is to be done with your child. There are two images, the first one for your child and the second one for you. Colour the images silently and mindfully. Make conscious choices about the colours you use, and notice how it feels to colour silently, including your sensations, your thoughts and emotions.

Once you have both finished colouring, ask your child questions about moments when he experienced compassion for others and what he did when he felt the compassion. Share your own observations of him when he was compassionate. You can also share your moments of being compassionate.

After the discussion, brainstorm three to five ways in which you could both be more compassionate towards your family and other beings.

Overleaf:
Child's Colouring Sheet (Activity 22)

Overleaf:
Parent's Colouring Sheet (Activity 22)

23. Likes and Dislikes

'No one ever likes the right person.' – Bret Easton Ellis

Our parents were very good at teaching us about managing likes and dislikes – sometimes to the point of overdoing it. As children, we did not have much choice over what was given to us. We learned to accept what was placed on the meal table, the clothes that were bought for us, or the places we were taken.

Once a week, I (Kathir) would be asked what I wanted to eat. However, my request was not always fulfilled. My sister liked different dishes from me and so my mother would cook what each of us liked on different days. There were days where we had to endure dishes that we did not like. This norm at home allowed us to practise acceptance gracefully over time, which led to insights about human likes and dislikes.

We learned that we may not always get what we like and what we do not like may be the thing that we get. The graceful acceptance of these two diametrically opposite experiences taught us another lesson, which was that the things we like may not always be wholesome and what we dislike may not always be unwholesome. There are many things that we dislike that can be very nourishing for our lives. These could be exercise, reading books, reading the news or eating healthy foods. And there are many things that we like that are unwholesome, like binge-watching movies, eating too much, eating too little, smoking, and device addictions.

Besides acceptance, there needs to be a healthy balance between our likes and dislikes. Many of us disliked studies in our younger years, but we enjoyed time with our schoolmates. This social connection motivated us to be in school. Similarly, you may not like tutoring your child after your long hours at work, but you do it anyway because it's your duty as a parent. If you enjoy the process, then that is considered a bonus.

Activity 23: Culture Appreciation

This is an experiment with different cultures' traditions as a family. By culture we refer to nationality, ethnicity, religious affiliation, etc. Start small and work your way upwards. The idea is to appreciate diversity, to become more inclusive, accommodating and respectful, and to enhance wisdom.

1. Milk Tasting: Buy a few flavoured milks, such as chocolate, banana or strawberry. Give a small amount of each flavour to every family member and ask everyone to taste and give a positive review of the milk in their own words. If your family does not like milk or is vegan, explore other flavoured drinks. Discuss how you can find positives in different types of drinks. Then extend this teaching to people, where each person is different and yet we can appreciate something in them.

2. Food Tasting: Go to a food court and order a variety of food or snacks from different cultures. Explore the smell, taste and visual presentation. Share what you like and dislike about the food but with respect. For example, it is fine to say, 'This is too spicy for my tastebuds', but it is disrespectful to say, 'This is awful.' Maybe explore a different cuisine each week. Expand the discussion to express gratitude for the people who bring the food to us, from the farmers to the stall-holders.

3. True or False: Come up with a list of interesting observations about each culture in your neighbourhood or country. This can include rituals, costumes, festivals, habits and customs. Write each observation on a piece of card, then place all the cards face-down on the table. Each person in the family picks one and states whether they think the statement is true or false. You can then discuss where the perception came from, how it helps or does not help to think in such a way and discuss the correct answers to the statements. See what insights develop from this activity.

4. Picture Game: Assemble a variety of photos from magazines or newspapers or print them from the net. These photos should represent different cultures in terms of their food, dress, words, activities, games, etc. Place all the images face-down on the table. Take turns to pick an image and share something about the culture it represents.

5. Culture Interview: As a family, draw up a list of questions that you always wanted to ask a person from a different culture. Once you are done, arrange a date to interview the person, either as a family or individually. To make it more challenging, each family member can choose a different culture group to interview.

24. Thought are Thoughts, Not You

'The beginning of wisdom is the definition of terms.' – Socrates

Communication is a very important part of human behaviour. We use words and string them into sentences to convey our thoughts and understand others. We communicate verbally by asking questions and making statements, and non-verbally through our body language and facial expressions.

One thing that happens naturally in language is the identification of what we feel with what we are. Here are a couple of examples to illustrate this phenomenon:

Experience	Internal statement
Feeling angry	I am angry.
Stomach rumbling due to hunger	I am hungry.
Body is heavier than recommended weight	I am fat.
People do not like me	I am ugly.

The interesting thing is that the verb 'am' functions like an equals sign (=). When I say that 'I am angry', it means 'I = angry', which is not true. You are who you are, who is far bigger than the anger you are feeling. Your anger is a transient feeling that will come and go.

So instead of identifying yourself with what you are feeling in the moment ('I am angry'), you could say, 'I am feeling angry' or, 'I am noticing that I am feeling anger.' Instead of saying, 'I am unwell', try saying, 'My stomach is aching.'

These mindful statements are a reflection of how you view your experiences. You are not your experiences, but you behold them in your awareness. It is similar to saying that you have a handbag rather than saying that you are a handbag.

By creating a more objective relationship with our experiences, we become wiser in the way we communicate with others and also in our internal dialogue with ourselves, which in turn reinforces our beliefs about ourselves.

Activity 24: Connecting the Dots

There are two images here, one for your child and one for you. Connect the dots to complete the pictures. You may choose to colour the pictures after you have connected all the dots. Once done, discuss with your child how her thoughts impact her emotions and belief system. You can use story books or other media to continue the conversation.

On a daily basis, try to help your child connect the dots on how when she says 'I am upset', she becomes that 'upset' person. Encourage her instead to say 'I am feeling ____' or 'My body is _____'. Help your child by consciously role-modelling this while helping them to rephrase their statements about their experiences.

MINDFULNESS

Overleaf:
Child's Colouring Sheet (Activity 24)

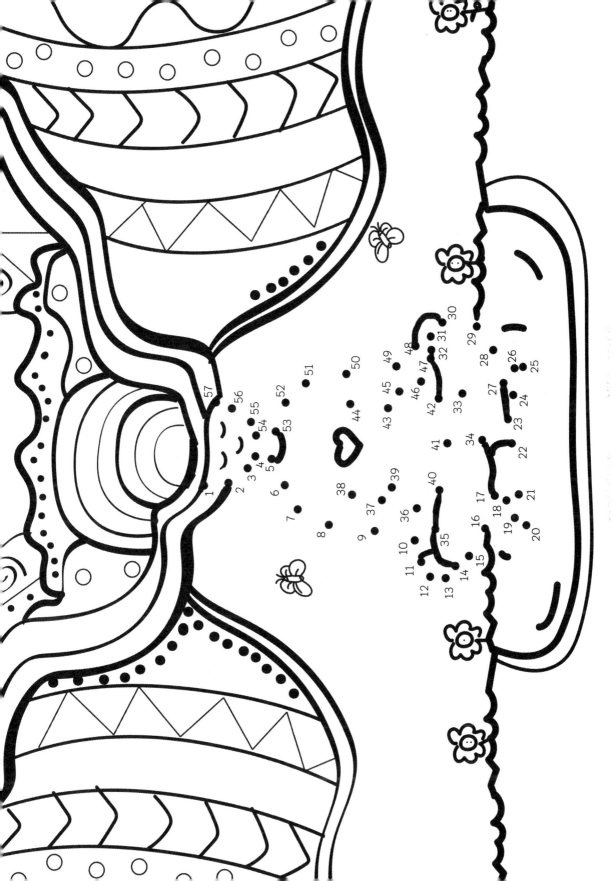

Overleaf:
Parent's Colouring Sheet (Activity 24)

25. Inviting All Experiences

'A wonderful gift may not be wrapped as you expect.' – Jonathan Lockwood Huie

As a kid, I (Kathir) was once very disappointed with a friend, who had embarrassed me that day in front of our class. The event kept playing in my head as I lay in bed, unable to sleep. I tried to push the thoughts out of my mind, and even tried to distract myself by reading a book, but the thoughts kept coming back.

This is how we usually manage our experiences and thoughts: we welcome the pleasant and reject the unpleasant. When we encounter things we do not like, we reject them or distract ourselves with other things. In fact, our lives can sometimes be filled with so many distractions that we forget what the most important things are.

In mindfulness, we learn to invite all experiences, because we know that they do not define who we are. We do not reject them nor look for ways to cope with them. We allow our thoughts

1. To be, or

2. Not to be, or

3. Appear in another form

Just as we invite all experiences, we also don't force them to stay. An experience may come, linger for some time, change and then leave. By having this realisation and practising mindfulness, we learn to cultivate the attitude of inviting all experiences without rejecting any.

Activity 25: The Guest House

Here is a poem called 'The Guest House' by Rumi for your reflection:

> *This being human is a guest house.*
> *Every morning a new arrival.*
>
> *A joy, a depression, a meanness,*
> *some momentary awareness comes*
> *as an unexpected visitor.*
>
> *Welcome and entertain them all!*
> *Even if they are a crowd of sorrows,*
> *who violently sweep your house*
> *empty of its furniture,*
> *still, treat each guest honourably.*
> *He may be clearing you out*
> *for some new delight.*
>
> *The dark thought, the shame, the malice.*
> *Meet them at the door laughing and invite*
> *them in.*
>
> *Be grateful for whatever comes.*
> *Because each has been sent*
> *as a guide from beyond.*

Now, we would like to invite you to interpret this poem. Write down what you think the poet meant by each line. You can include your personal experiences in your reflection. For example, this is how we might interpret the first line of the poem:

> *This being human is a guest house.*
>
> A guest house is a metaphor for our humanity and our experience. An opportunity to experience something new in our lives.
>
> Our mind, too, is like a guest house. All types of guests, such as our thoughts and emotions, can drop by. But like the guests who come and go, these thoughts and emotions shall also leave. They come and go. They do not stay.

Feel free to expand on this and reflect on the rest of the poem.

26. Forgiveness

'Real forgiveness in close relationships is never easy. It can't be rushed or engineered.' – Sharon Salzberg

Forgiveness is about not feeling angry and not wanting to punish a person who has committed a mistake. Forgiveness helps you to let go of anger that you could be holding within you.

We discussed earlier how your emotions impact your body. Anger impacts areas of your head, chest and hands, as if to prepare the body for a fight. When you are unable to forgive someone, it stays stored in your body. This can cause health problems such as digestive issues, headaches, muscle aches and tension.

If you have not been forgiven for a mistake you made, this can prevent you from extending your benevolence towards those individuals. Sometimes mistakes made by someone are so grave that you can't forgive the person. For example, that person might have betrayed your trust, cheated on you or hurt you for no reason. Such acts are very hard to forgive. However, time will heal the pain, and there is always still the possibility of you forgiving such a person in the future.

This also applies within the family. It's essential that we teach children to forgive. Many a time, children learn to forgive from their parents. Let them know that committing a mistake is normal. What's important is that they learn from the mistake. Of course, we are talking about honest mistakes and not about wilfully doing the wrong thing.

Beyond forgiveness, we also need the courage to apologise when we commit a mistake. The courage to apologise can also sometimes create an opportunity to be forgiven. It is fine for you to apologise to your child if you made a mistake as the child learns that apologies do not depend on authority, status or age.

The ability to apologise, which is to recognise our own shortcomings, can also be a mark of humility. When children learn to reflect, apologise when they are in the wrong, and forgive others when others make mistakes, they grow up to be humble and compassionate.

Here is a Forgiveness Meditation from the mindfulness tradition that can help us cultivate the ability to forgive. We encourage you to meditate on this as a family:

> May I be able to pardon all living beings
> May they always be able to pardon me
> May there be friendship among all living beings
> May I have no hatred of anyone

Activity 26: Be Forgiving

This activity is to be done with your child. There are two images on the following pages, one for your child and one for you. Colour the images silently and mindfully, taking note of your sensations, thoughts and emotions.

Once you have both finished, ask your child questions about any incident where he was forgiving towards others. You can also share your own observations of him when he was forgiving. Also explore situations with him when he could not forgive someone or when someone did not forgive him. Ask questions to understand his thoughts, emotions, bodily sensations, and actions for each situation. You can also share your own moments of being forgiving, non-forgiving and where you were not forgiven.

Overleaf:
Child's Colouring Sheet (Activity 26)

Overleaf:
Parent's Colouring Sheet (Activity 26)

27. Start and End the Day Intentionally

'Every journey begins with the first step of articulating the intention, and then becoming the intention.' – Bryant McGill

Starting and ending your day intentionally is a good habit to cultivate. It allows the attitudes of mindfulness and its insights to pervade your thoughts throughout the day.

You can do this by sitting on your bed in the morning and thinking about what matters to you as a human being, which probably centres around your well-being and your family's well-being. It is important that you set the intention that the day is going to be in the mission of serving yourself, your family and others. Encourage your children to do the same.

If you happen to share your bed with another person, make sure you don't start the day with a disagreement, argument or fight. If you know that the other person is going to start one, be prepared to defuse this respectfully and calmly. Take a pause to be first with yourself. It is better for you to talk about this after setting the intention for the day.

At the end of the day, before you rest your head on your pillow, think about what went well in the day, what you are grateful for, and how others have contributed to it. Let go of the day by forgiving yourself and others through the Forgiveness Meditation (page 168). With that warmth in your heart and mind, go to bed.

It is important that the space you rest in daily resonates calm, peace and joy. Treat it with respect, like it's a sanctuary. Avoid arguing and fighting in bed. If you need to talk about something that is likely to make you or your partner uncomfortable, have that conversation away from your bed and away from your children. We recommend resolving any disagreements before going to bed. If need be, agree on a time to talk about it the following day.

Activity 27: Grounding

Start of the day

When you awake, sit silently for a couple of minutes just noticing your breath. When you place your feet on the floor, notice the sensations in your feet. When you stand up, close your eyes and stand there for a while noticing your body weight, your bodily sensations and your breath.

Now, letting go of noticing the body, shift your attention to your intention. Set your intention for the day. You may choose to use your purpose statement created earlier or create a new intention below:

Open your eyes and continue the day feeling grounded.

Noon

Around noon, or whenever you can during the day, close your eyes and sit or stand silently for a minute. Just be aware of your breath. Notice every in-breath and out-breath. After this, walk around the office or home or school as mindfully as you can. Notice how your body responds as you walk.

Evening

If possible, before dinner, carry out some activities that engage the whole family. For example, you could solve a math problem or some riddles together. Find fun ways to engage with one another.

Night

When you are about to turn in for the night, stand beside your bed, close your eyes and notice your body weight, your bodily sensations and your breath. Then, sit on your bed silently for a couple of minutes. Recall one positive or meaningful moment in the day or maybe even consider doing your Forgiveness Meditation (see page 168). You may then sleep feeling grounded.

Teach these grounding activities to your children too. You may reduce the times so that they can achieve it. For example, silent sitting can be for 30 seconds instead of a few minutes. If you read to your children daily, consider doing this right after they have finished their grounding practice.

28. Device Detox

'Every form of addiction is bad, no matter whether the narcotic be alcohol, morphine or idealism.' – Carl Jung

Devices have become part of our lives in an unprecedented way. Children today even need their laptops or electronic tablets as part of their school learning. It's safe to say that some of us wouldn't mind losing our wallet or purse but not our smartphone. In many ways, we should be grateful to the inventors of these devices for making our lives more convenient.

However, the drawback is that technology seems to be taking over our lives. We simply can't stay away from our devices. Everywhere you go, you see couples, families and children glued to their mobile devices, ignoring the people they are with. Parents often hand their devices to their children to keep them entertained during car rides or mealtimes. It has become an addiction.

While it might appear that devices have taken us hostage, it is actually the opposite. It is us who are choosing to be with these devices, not the other way around. Being mindful requires that we use devices with discretion. Instead of being drawn to the devices as an autopilot behaviour, try to make it a conscious choice. For example, set specific timings for using devices, and try to institute a no-devices rule at the dinner table. The same rules should apply to the parents and children alike.

Activity 28: Complete the Sentence

To harness our energy that would otherwise go into our devices, we need to have activities to stay connected with one another. This does not mean that children should not be left alone to get bored. Boredom is actually good for creativity. However, long periods of boredom will naturally incline the child to move towards their devices.

Try out this activity, where you take turns to complete the sentences.

- I would like to . . .
- If I were president, I would . . .
- If I were a superhero, I would . . .
- If my mind could . . .
- If a miracle were to happen tomorrow, . . .

Create your own prompts, and try out other games as well, such as Sudoku, word puzzles or brain teasers. Stay connected with one another, not your devices.

29. Using the 'Why' Question Sparingly

'Judge a man by his questions rather than by his answers.' – Voltaire

We can learn quite a lot from psychotherapists and counsellors about asking questions. These professionals tend to avoid asking certain types of questions that are not helpful. One such type of questions are 'why' questions.

'Why' questions are usually asked with the intention of quickly getting to the root cause of a problem and to move the discussion forward. They can make people feel judged, challenged, defensive or even lost. This happens with children too.

I (Sunita) have noticed that in families where there are marital issues, 'why' questions tend to appear very frequently in conversation, especially when discussing challenging issues. Consider these two pairs of questions:

Why did you go there?

vs

What was your desire in going there?

Why are you late?

vs

How come you are late?

You'll notice that the 'why' questions sound more judgemental and interrogative. You'll also notice that the 'why' questions can be easily converted into 'what' or 'how' questions. Phrased in this way, the questions allow people to think about the issue more deeply and descriptively, to label their emotions, and to express their thoughts without feeling defensive.

It is also important that you do not ask questions when you are not interested in knowing the answer. If you have already made up your mind about how the conversation is going to go, then asking questions is quite meaningless. Your children won't want to answer your questions because they know it's not going to be worth their effort. Questions have to come from a place of curiosity and genuinely wanting to understand the members of your family.

Activity 29: The 19 Questions Game

In mindfulness, we want to be aware that asking too many questions can make individuals feel like they are being interrogated. At the same time, we want to respectfully ask meaningful questions. As such, we recommend that when you ask questions, do not go beyond 19 questions.

We like the number 19 not because it is special but simply because the numbers 1 and 9 amaze us. For example, anything multiplied or divided by 1 is always the original number. It is also the first natural number after zero. As for the number 9, when you multiply any number by 9, the answer that you get can be reduced back to the number 9. For example, 9 x 3 = 27 and 2 + 7 = 9. Try it for yourself and see.

This activity is for the whole family, with each person being assigned a role. First, get seated in a circle.

Artist: One person takes on the role of the Artist. She has to think of something that she wishes to communicate to the family. This could be what she is thinking about now, or a recent experience, or something related to her hobby. She then draws this out on a flip-chart or any large piece of paper. No words or letters are allowed in the drawing. Once the drawing is complete, the other family members will try and guess what it represents by asking questions to the Artist.

Question Tracker: One person takes on the role of the Question Tracker. His task is to keep track of the number of questions that have been asked. Once the family has asked 10 questions, he will inform everyone that they have only 9 questions remaining. He will remind the group again when there only 3 questions remaining. The Question Tracker also participates in the questioning.

Curious Family: The rest of the players take on the role of a Curious Family to ask questions to understand and guess what the Artist has drawn. The rule is that only closed-ended questions (e.g. Yes/No, Wrong/Right) are allowed. The Curious Family can ask a maximum of 19 questions.

Once someone manages to correctly guess what the Artist has drawn, the game ends. Otherwise, at the end of the 19 questions, the Artist will reveal the answer. The family can then choose to share their personal insights from the activity.

Here is an example of a drawing and the questions that were asked by the Curious Family, and the Artist's replies:

Artist's drawing

No.	Curious Family's questions	Artist's replies
1	Is this a family picture?	Yes.
2	Is it our family?	Yes.
3	Was this a recent thing?	Yes, last year.
4	Was it an important day?	Yes.
5	Which date was it?	19 November 2019.
6	What are they doing?	Going somewhere.
7	Is that an apple tree?	Yes.
8	Is that important in the picture?	Not really.
9	Then why did you draw it?	I cannot answer that question.
10	Are they going out?	Yes.
11	Are they going to eat?	No.
12	On 19 November 2019, we went overseas, correct?	Yes.
13	Is this picture showing the day we left for the airport?	Yes. You got the answer!

30. Respect for All

'I speak to everyone in the same way, whether he is the garbage man or the president of the university.' – Albert Einstein

Self-respect and respecting others allows us to nurture appreciation for others and ourselves. This appreciation stems from the vision that we are all simple human beings. Behind the CEO, the boss, the domestic helper, the president, the janitor, the nurse and the taxi driver, there is a simple human being who wants to be happy. Anchoring ourselves to this fact allows us to treat everyone with respect. Children watch how we respect others and ourselves and learn to do the same.

Respect for others can be shown through three ways – SAT:

- **S**peech: the words and statements we make and the tone of our voice
- **A**ctions: the things we do for people
- **T**houghts: the thoughts and rationale we have for our speech and actions

Our thoughts in any situation influence our speech and actions. And behind those thoughts are our beliefs about the people we are interacting with. Our preconceptions about them may play out in the way we treat them.

When you speak in a different tone, e.g. a sharp and frustrated tone, your child notices. She learns that in certain situations she can speak in that way too.

For example, if we were to be rude to the taxi driver when he takes us on a wrong route, she learns that she too can be rude and disrespect others when they make mistakes. In the same scenario, if we had shared our disappointment about the wrong route but forgiven the cabbie, she would learn how to voice her feelings in a respectful manner and to forgive others as a way forward.

As we practise mindfulness, we become more aware of these biases that influence the way we show respect to others.

One of the most challenging situations, where we struggle to maintain respect for others, is when we have been disrespected. When this happens, the mind chooses to do the same to that person in a tit-for-tat. At such times, take a pause before responding mindfully. If you are able to, practise Coping Breathing Space. This will help you have a respectful conversation where you do not become spiteful, hurtful or vengeful.

Activity 30: Respect All Beings and Things

Here are two images, the first one for your child and the second one for you. Colour the images silently and mindfully. Make conscious choices in picking the colours to use. Notice how it feels to colour silently, including your sensations, thoughts and emotions.

Once you have both finished, ask your child questions about occasions when she saw you respecting others. Then, share with her examples of times when you noticed her respecting others.

Talk about what respect looks like in terms of SAT. Discuss how you can both do more to respect all beings. Start with the other people in the family and then go outwards to the extended family, teachers, friends, neighbours, plants and animals. What are the SATs that show respect to all beings?

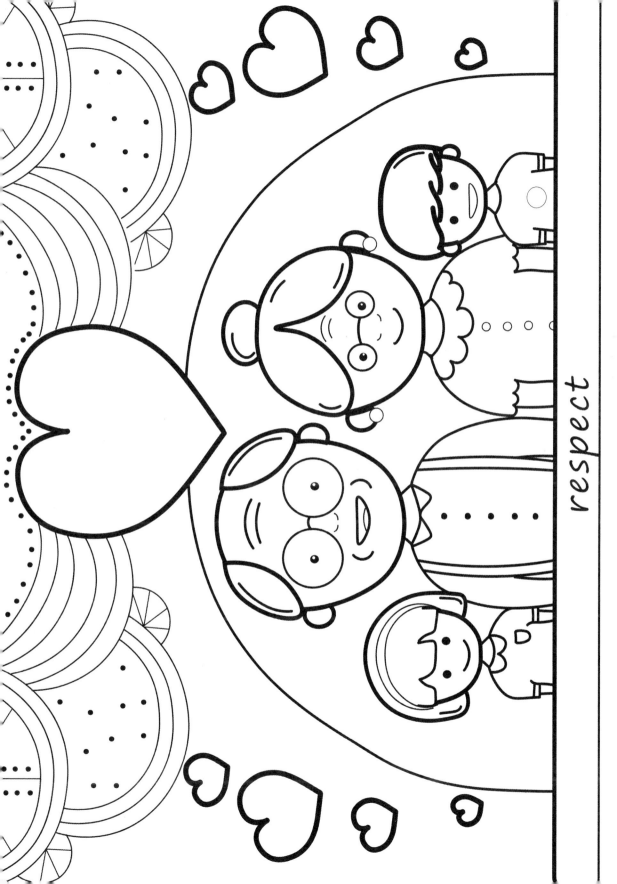

respect

Overleaf:
Child's Colouring Sheet (Activity 30)

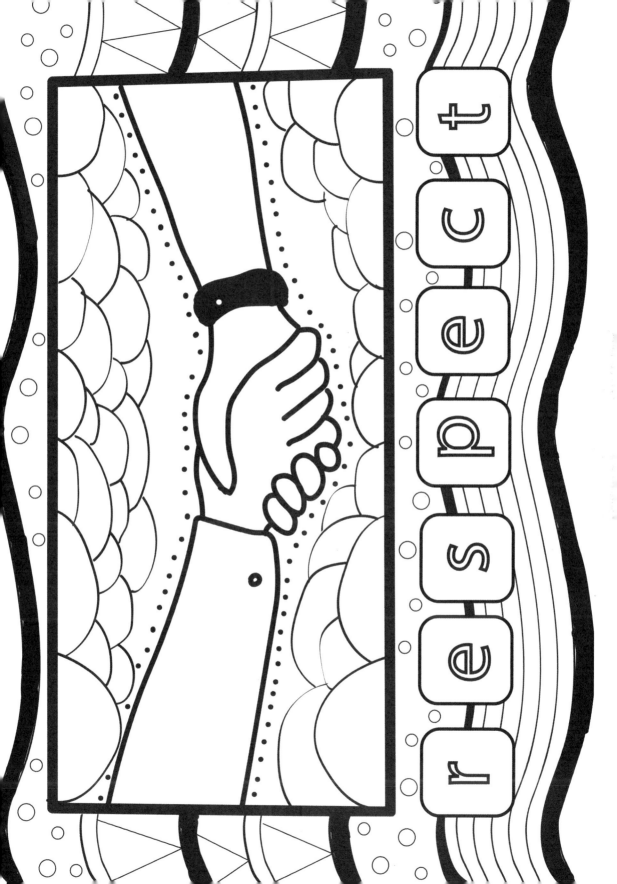

respect

Overleaf:
Parent's Colouring Sheet (Activity 30)

Mindful Movement

The purpose of this practice is to bring awareness, explore boundaries and uncover insights that may arise through mindful movement. This practice can be done together with your child. You may also take advantage of video practice files (available on the internet) to guide you.

1. While seated or standing, gently bring awareness to your body.

2. Close your eyes and scan your body from your feet to the top of your head.

3. Open your eyes and explore any movements and bring your awareness to that movement.

4. Turn your head to the left, centre, right, centre, upwards, centre, down and centre and notice the movements, stretches and sensations as you move.

5. Roll your shoulders forward slowly for 3-5 counts and then backward, and observe the bodily sensations.

6. Raise your left arm slowly towards the direction of the ceiling and notice the sensations as you move it. Gently lower it while noticing the sensations. Repeat the action with your right arm.

7. Raise both your arms to the sky and notice the sensations. Slowly bring them down and notice the difference in the blood flow and any other sensations.

8. Slowly move your hips to the left and the right and notice the sensations that the movements bring.

9. Raise your left foot off the floor as high as you can and notice the movements and sensations. Repeat the motion with your right foot.

10. Do a slow stretch of your whole body and notice the bodily sensations.

11. After you have finished, notice the sensations of the body in stillness.

12. When you're done, continue with the rest of the day with awareness of your body in movement.

CHAPTER 8

What is the Way Forward?

Congratulations on having completed this book. We started by sharing with you an episode of two families in a beautiful park. One family was intent on enjoying the resources that were available in the park while the other was intent on contributing to these resources. Our lives are constantly at play with these two energies, consuming and contributing. One without the other makes life empty. Perhaps we can look at them as two ends of a continuum:

Consume ⟷ Contribute

By finding the balance between these two energies, we find our place in the world, and become happier as a result. And to find that balance, we begin by bringing mindfulness into our families.

We've seen that mindfulness has the ability to significantly impact families as it is a form of psychological capital. The responsibility for creating a mindful family rests on the parents, and hence it is important that you appreciate mindfulness first before letting the benefits pervade the life of your children.

Through mindfulness, you will become more purposeful and wise, know more about yourself, and free yourself from stress, anxiety and burnout. You will still experience stress from time to time, naturally, but your response has changed.

When mindfulness is practised as a family, it benefits the children immensely. Instead of the children learning mindfulness like an extra-curricular class, they learn it from their parents, who practise and model it. The children benefit from the seeds of wisdom planted in their minds at a tender age. These seeds then sprout into trees that will guide them in their adult lives to make wiser decisions that help themselves, others and the world they live in.

The mindfulness skills that your children learn will also help them cope with any current challenges. For example, they are poised to use mindfulness to improve their academic performance. But to us, more than anything else, if your children discover themselves to be simple human beings, that is the greatest realisation.

We hope the activities in the book bring value to your whole family. Practise the activities together to discover your being, align your sense of doing with your being, and allow wisdom to manifest.

That said, finishing this book does not mean the journey is over. Wisdom is an evolving understanding of yourself, others and the world over time. The key to sustaining mindfulness in your family lies in the practice of mindfulness. Nothing else is needed.

If you are interested in taking the next step into mindfulness, we encourage you to participate in a formal mindfulness programme in your city. Through these programmes, which are typically run over 8 weeks, you'll be able to deepen your understanding of mindfulness practices in a structured manner.

Thank you for picking up this book, and for your courage and willingness to try out these activities. We wish you and your family happiness and well-being.

And most importantly,

May you be well
May you be happy
May you be healthy
May you be free from distress.

This is all we wish for you.

Loving Kindness Meditation

This practice expands your capacity for kindness by cultivating heartfulness and self- and other-love. In this meditation, allow yourself to switch from the usual mode of doing to a mode of being. You can also use an audio practice file (available on the internet) to guide you.

Sit comfortably with your back upright and close your eyes.

Become aware of the movement of your breath, the in-breath and the out-breath. Notice every single inhalation and exhalation for a couple of minutes.

Now bring to mind someone for whom you have deep feelings of love. Notice your feelings for them arise in your body. It may be a smile that spreads across your face, or your chest becomes warm. Whatever the effects, allow them to be felt.

Now let go of this person in your mind, and see if you can offer loving kindness to yourself, by letting these words become your words mentally:

May I be well
May I be happy
May I be healthy
May I be free from distress

Notice the feelings that arise and let them be.

When you are comfortable, try offering loving kindness to someone who supports you, someone who has always been on your side. Bring this person to mind, imagine them sitting across from you, and let these words become your words mentally:

May you be well
May you be happy
May you be healthy
May you be free from distress

Once your feelings flow easily to a loved one, turn your attention to someone you have difficulty with. We suggest that It's best not to start with the most difficult person in your life, but perhaps someone who brings up feelings of irritation or annoyance. See if you can let these words become your words mentally as you keep this person in your awareness:

May you be well
May you be happy
May you be healthy
May you be free from distress

Notice the sensations and feelings that arise within you. See if you can let them just be.

Bring to mind the broader community you are part of. You might imagine your family, your workmates, your staff, your neighbours, or you might even fan out your attention to include all persons and creatures on the planet.

Include yourself in this offering of loving kindness, as you let these words become your words mentally:

May all be well
May all be happy
May all be healthy
May all be free from distress

Notice the sensations and feelings that arise within you. Sit with them until you are ready to end the practice with the following words:

May all overcome their obstacles
May all see goodness
May all attain their cherished desires
May all be happy always
May I be able to forgive all living beings
May they always be able to forgive me
May there be friendship among all living beings
May I have no hatred of anyone

And as we end this practice, open your eyes and continue the day with kindness, gratitude and love for all.

Loving Kindness Meditation

With children, this practice may be shortened and guided by the parent. We have a recommended script below, but feel free to adapt it as you feel necessary.

Sit comfortably with your back upright.

Become aware of the movement of your breath, the in-breath and the out-breath. Notice every single inhalation and exhalation for a couple of minutes.

Bring to mind someone you love or like very much and see if you can offer loving kindness to yourself, by saying these words mentally:

May I be well
May I be happy
May I be healthy
May I be free from any kind of pain

Now try offering loving kindness to someone who supports you by saying these words mentally:

May you be well
May you be happy
May you be healthy
May you be free from any kind of pain

Now think of someone you dislike or have difficulties with. See if you can offer them loving kindness by saying these words mentally:

May you be well
May you be happy
May you be healthy
May you be free from any kind of pain

And now think of the entire planet, including your family, your friends, all persons and all creatures, including yourself, and see if you can offer them loving kindness by saying these words mentally:

May all be well
May all be happy
May all be healthy
May all be free from any kind of pain

Notice the sensations and feelings that arise within you. Sit with them for a few moments until you are ready to end the practice with the following words:

May all overcome their obstacles

May all see goodness

May all attain their cherished desires

May all be happy always

May I be able to forgive all living beings

May they always be able to forgive me

May there be friendship among all living beings

May I have no hatred of anyone

* * *

And as we end this practice, open your eyes
and continue the day with kindness,
gratitude and love for all.

© 2020 Marshall Cavendish International (Asia) Pte Ltd, K. Kathirasan and Sunita Rai

Published in 2020 by Marshall Cavendish Editions
An imprint of Marshall Cavendish International

All rights reserved

Other Marshall Cavendish Offices:
Marshall Cavendish Corporation, 800 Westchester Ave, Suite N-641, Rye Brook, NY 10573, USA • Marshall Cavendish International (Thailand) Co Ltd, 253 Asoke, 16th Floor, Sukhumvit 21 Road, Klongtoey Nua, Wattana, Bangkok 10110, Thailand • Marshall Cavendish (Malaysia) Sdn Bhd, Times Subang, Lot 46, Subang Hi-Tech Industrial Park, Batu Tiga, 40000 Shah Alam, Selangor Darul Ehsan, Malaysia

Marshall Cavendish is a registered trademark of Times Publishing Limited

National Library Board, Singapore Cataloguing in Publication Data
Name(s): Kathirasan, K. | Rai, Sunita (Psychologist) author.
Title: Mindfulness for the Family : A parent-child workbook for greater awareness and stronger relationships / Kathirasan K and Dr Sunita Rai.
Description: Singapore : Marshall Cavendish Editions, [2020]
Identifier(s): OCN 1178715837 | ISBN 978-981-4893-66-4 (paperback)
Subject(s): LCSH: Parenting–Psychological aspects. | Parent and child–Psychological aspects. | Mindfulness (Psychology)
Classification: DDC 649.1019–dc23

Colouring sheets illustrated by Hernie Khames-Martin, Magan Lam Wan Kay and Girinandhini d/o Govindharaju

Printed in Singapore